PICK UP YOUR SOCKS

... and other skills growing children need!

By Elizabeth Crary
Illustrations by Pati Casebolt

PARENTING PRESS, INC.
Seattle, Washington

The author gratefully acknowledges the help of class members, friends, family, and Parenting Press, Inc. staff, particularly Shari Steelsmith and Laurene Hartvigsen, in the development and editing of this book.

I am particularly thankful to the following people for examples and feedback: Jean Illsley Clarke, Fred Crary, Lora and Charles Deinken.

ISBN 0-943990-52-1 (paperback)
ISBN 0-943990-53-X (library binding)

LC 89-62656

Parenting Press, Inc.
P.O. Box 75267
Seattle, WA 98175
www.ParentingPress.com

TABLE OF CONTENTS

Introduction

Pick Up Your Socks ... *and other skills growing children need* is about encouraging responsibility. Sometimes parents unconsciously expect their child to embody the finest qualities in each of their friends' children—without their accompanying irritations. Most people, both parents and children, are responsible in some areas, and not responsible in others. This book will help you recognize where your child is and then build on the abilities that already exist.

The idea for this book began shortly after my first book—*Without Spanking or Spoiling: A Practical Approach to Toddler and Preschool Guidance*—was published. People began asking me for a book about school-aged children. The thread running through their questions was—"How can I encourage responsibility in my children?"

I began to talk with parents about what they would like to know, and what tools and information they found most helpful. Many parents had similar concerns—discipline, household chores, homework, and independent living skills. However, they differed dramatically in what approach was useful and what they expected from their children.

My intention with *Pick Up Your Socks* is to provide you with a variety of information. You can adapt the material to your own concerns and issues. Some of the material, particularly on the development of responsibility, comes from my own observation and research. Some information is adapted from other professionals. Much of the information also comes from parents themselves.

Because parents, as well as children, learn in different ways, I have accommodated different learning styles in the text. Some people do well simply reading a book. Others like language they can use modelled for them. Still others need to practice the information before they understand it. For the people wanting language, I have included lots of examples. The examples come from family, friends, colleagues, and parents I work with. The names and details have been changed, but the situations are common. For people who want to practice the ideas, I included exercises. The exercises give you a chance to practice the techniques before you use them with your children. I have added possible answers for most exercises. They are not the only *right* answers, but simply a place to start.

This book was originally designed for parents of school-aged children. However, during field testing I found it had a much wider appeal. Parents of pre-school children and teenagers find the tools and ideas useful. Parents of grown children found ideas to help with problems they continue to face. One woman even remarked, "This is great! It works with husbands as well as kids."

Pick up Your Socks looks at encouraging responsibility. It is a skill people develop over time, not a trait they are born with. The process of becoming responsible is a lifelong journey. With some people the journey is light and breezy, with others it takes more planning and follow through. You are a valuable person regardless of the style with which your child chooses to travel. I hope the information you receive from *Pick up Your Socks* will make your journey, and your children's, more enjoyable.

CHAPTER 1: BEFORE YOU BEGIN

Developing responsibility in children is important to most of today's parents. Parents repeatedly ask, "How can I get my child to be responsible for—tidying her room, doing schoolwork, taking out the trash, getting to school on time, feeding the pet, practicing the piano, ...?" On and on goes the list. Before we look at how to encourage responsibility, we need to examine what it means, and what is appropriate to expect of children at different ages.

Responsibility vs. obedience

Parents agree that they want their children to be responsible, but what responsibility means to each parent varies dramatically. For me, the distinction between responsibility and obedience is "who decides the child will do the task" and "where the motivation for completing it originates."

With obedience, the child is expected to do what he or she is told. Obedience needs no agreement on the part of the child. The decision and motivation come from outside the child. Responsibility, however, involves the child's acceptance of the task and motivation for finishing the job. The difference between internal and external motivation can be seen in the example below.

We lived in a small town while the twins were in school. Jeanne never gave us a spot of trouble while she was growing up. She always did what we asked without questioning it. She was a delight to have around. Johnny was another story. He always did what he wanted. When he agreed to do something, it would be done; however, if he didn't agree, you might as well forget it.

When it came time for college, both children wanted to go to the state university. Although the school was good in some fields, it had a reputation as a party school. We thought Jeanne would be fine, but we were worried about sending Johnny. We thought the temptations might be too great for Johnny since we had to discipline him several times for driving across the state line with friends to get liquor.

As it turned out, our concern was misplaced. Johnny had learned how to make decisions for himself—and he wanted to study chemistry. Jeanne, on the other hand, had always done what she was told. Now people told her that to be popular, she needed to "party." And party she did!

As I think back on what happened, I don't think Jeanne was "rebelling" the way some children do. I think we just didn't help her develop the skills she needed to make her own decisions and motivate herself.

Responsibility involves both personal decision and motivation. When children do what they are told by a parent, friend, police officer, or teacher, whether they agree or not, that is obedience. Usually a person obeys to avoid punishment or to be cooperative for the common good. People act responsibly when they choose what to do and motivate themselves to get it done.

Children need to learn both obedience and responsibility. Obedience is appropriate in many situations. To function effectively as a society, we must have some group rules. If we each decided separately which side of the road to drive on, we would have chaos. But thoughtless obedience in all situations can be just as dangerous as thoughtless independence. There are certain decisions about drugs, sex, politics, and honesty that people must make for themselves. Personal responsibility is needed, or people lose their individuality or humanity. In the most extreme cases of blind obedience, children may get involved in cults or street gangs, and countries operate like Germany under Hitler's command when people "only did what they were told."

Components of responsibility

There are three parts to responsibility: understanding the task, accepting accountability for the task, and motivating one's self. Without all three of these components, the response becomes painful groping or mere obedience.

Understanding the task involves knowing both what is to be done and how to do it. What looks like laziness or incompetence may result from not understanding a task. Sometimes a child will agree to a task, and later learn that his parent believed he agreed to something else.

Tommy was lying in the middle of a sea of crayons and toys, drawing a picture of a space ship. His mother came in and reminded him that his favorite show would start in 10 minutes, and he needed "to clean up his mess." He agreed to clean up before watching television.

Shortly he stopped drawing, picked up the papers and crayons, and took them to his room. When he returned, he turned on the TV. His mother came in and yelled at him for not cleaning his mess. He said, "I did too." He cleaned up the crayons and drawing paper. However, his mother had expected him also to pick up all the toys.

In some cases both parent and child agree to a task, but the child does not have all the information needed. This is illustrated by Marianne's experience.

Company was coming for supper. I was planning to leave work early, put a turkey in the oven, and clean the house. When I left work, the car's engine would not start, so a friend and I pushed the car across the street to a service station. They said they could fix the car but it would take two or three hours. I told them, "Fine" and called my daughter Sandy (age 11).

I told Sandy to take the turkey from the refrigerator and put it in a roasting bag. Then to put the turkey, bag and all, into a roasting pan, and put it in the oven. I also asked her to clean the bathroom and tidy the living room. When I got home she had done exactly as I said. Unfortunately, I neglected to tell her to turn on the oven. It seems crazy that she didn't know to turn on the oven, but she is the youngest and had never cooked at all.

The challenge of understanding a task involves clear communication between parent and child. The adult needs to indicate the scope of the job and the standard for completion. This is easiest when the parent knows at what level the child has been successful in the past and explains the information accordingly. The parent also needs to encourage the child to ask questions to clarify the task.

Acceptance of the task shifts the job from obedience to responsibility. Before you *ask* a child to do something—"*will you please help me put away the groceries?*"—you need to be clear about whether the child has a choice. If the child has no choice, do not ask! Tell him or her what you want: "Tracy, come help me put the groceries away." With obedience, the parent needs to apply whatever motivation and supervision is needed for compliance.

If the child has a choice, he or she can begin to exercise responsibility. All parents would like children to willingly accept and do all the tasks parents want done. Few children, however, want to work as much as their parents wish they would. Some parents offer children the choice and then try to pressure them into accepting the task if they say "No." The question then becomes what *should* the child do if he or she is unwilling to help? Should he say "Yes" when he will probably do it poorly or forget to do it? Or, should he say "No" and face displeasure at the beginning? Many parents find they prefer to be told "No," when they ask a child to do something, rather than find out later that he or she did not do it.

Some parents find it difficult to permit children to choose whether or not they will do a task. One woman finds it helpful to remind herself that the ability to say "No" to jobs is a healthy adult trait. Her story is described below.

I can remember as a child my parents were involved in everything—church, PTA, scouts, school board, Little League, swim team, and politics. Any time someone asked them to help they always agreed, regardless of how little time they had. People thought we children were lucky to have parents so involved with everything, but it didn't feel that way to us kids. There was never any time for us.

Mother often complained that she didn't have time to do the reading and sewing she liked to do. I guess they never had any time for themselves, either. I decided, as a teen, that when I grew up I wouldn't let people pressure me into doing things I didn't want to do.

When I ask my kids to do a task, and they say "No," I remember that they are practicing skills they will need to be competent adults.

Clearly, there are some jobs which children must do and others which they

I did clean up my room!

may decline. In each family the optional jobs and required jobs will vary. If children are to learn to think for themselves, they must have practice saying "No."

Ability to motivate self. Young children are totally dependent upon older people for support and information. As children grow older, one of the parent's jobs is to shift the source of the child's motivation from the parent (external motivation) to the child (internal motivation), and to help the child develop the ability to discipline himself or herself for long-term benefits rather than short-term gain. This shift is one that comes partly with age and partly with experience.

Parents can help a young child by offering encouragement in the form of praise or reward. However, as the child grows, the source of encouragement should shift gradually until the child can motivate himself or herself. In the next chapter, we will present several ways to help children learn to do this.

It is also helpful to understand which direction you want your children to go. Look at your children's behavior and see what they are doing responsibly. The following exercise (Exercise 1-1) is an easy way to begin identifying responsible behavior.

EXERCISE 1-1: Identifying Responsibility

Instructions: Read each situation below and decide if you think it shows responsibility, obedience, or neither. **R** = responsibility, **O** = obedience, **N** = neither.

_____ 1. Matthew washes the dishes promptly because he knows he cannot watch TV until they are done.

_____ 2. Jane loves to read. As soon as she gets home from school on Monday she starts her reading assignment, which isn't due until the end of the week.

_____ 3. Emily wants to be on the swim team. Each day she goes to the pool and practices.

_____ 4. Edmund promised to bring his school friend a book, but forgot.

_____ 5. Jennifer's father gave her a bike before he left on a month-long trip and told her he would teach her how to ride it when he got back. She does not like bikes, but each day she practices a little so she can surprise him when he gets back.

_____ 6. Mark has begun to practice his spelling words by himself at home. If he gets an A on his next spelling test, Mom will take him to McDonald's™ for lunch.

_____ 7. Sally hates spelling. Her mother says she must do better and helps her practice spelling each night. When they are done spelling, Sally's mother reads her a story.

Possible answers:
1. Obedience, unless Matthew would wash dishes promptly without restriction. **2.** Responsibility, she could read something else. **3.** Responsibility, Emily goes without prompting. **4.** Neither obedience nor responsibility. **5.** Neither obedience nor responsibility; no agreement was made. **6.** Responsibility.
7. Obedience.

Levels of responsibility

People, both children and adults, learn to be responsible in small steps. There are three levels of responsibility for a task.

Helps with the task. The first level is for the child to assist with the task. In this stage, children learn how to do the task. When first beginning a new task, many children (whether 6 or 16) need moral support and physical presence.

I remember teaching Paul to set the table. He would stand beside me and watch everything I did. When I put the knife down, he put the knife down, and so on for the forks, plates, and napkins. After he learned the placement of things, he still wanted my presence until <u>he</u> was sure he knew how.

Later, when he was a teen, he wished to order a phone. He wanted me to place the order for him. I felt he was capable of ordering, although he did not think so. We resolved the situation by his making the call while I listened on another phone to answer questions and support him.

Needs reminding or supervision. At this level, children have most of the general information they need for the task. However, they may forget something or need to be reminded that it is their turn.

Maria was always a very helpful child—willing to pitch in when needed, but she could never get it all right at first. For example, if she were setting the table she would often forget something—napkins, spoons, or glasses. I would come and help her figure out what was missing. Only after she had done the same task many, many times could I depend on her doing it right.

Does the task alone. The third level of responsibility is independence. Not only does the child do the job alone, completely and satisfactorily, he or she no longer needs reminding. This is the level we all work toward.

When Molly was two, she was very interested in clothes and spent a lot of time trying to dress herself. She couldn't do it alone, but she didn't want my help. I sewed pull-on pants and loose tops so she could put on her clothes easily. Ever since then, incredible as it seems, she has dressed herself without help. She even chooses reasonable combinations of clothes.

You can practice identifying levels of responsibility in Exercise 1-2: Levels of Responsibility.

Parents' expectations. A child's level of responsibility depends upon the development and age of the child and upon the parents' expectations. Some parents are unwilling to turn over responsibility to a child. In other cases, it never occurs to them to let the child be responsible.

I dressed Ricky every day until he was more than four years old. One day, my son and I were visiting his friend Martin. Martin had a two-year-old sister who was dressing herself as we came in. I was amazed and curious to know if Ricky could dress himself. The next day I gave him the chance and found he was both willing and able to dress himself. I had never offered him the chance. I wonder how long I would have dressed him before thinking of it myself.

Parents convey their expectations both verbally and non-verbally. In this example, the message was non-verbal. The parents never offered Ricky the

EXERCISE 1-2: Levels of Responsibility

Instructions: Read each of the items below and mark what level of responsibility you think it displays:
A = needs assistance; S = needs supervision; I = works independently.

____ 1. Gerri takes the trash out as soon as she is reminded.

____ 2. Dana vacuums the house on Saturday before going out to play.

____ 3. Evan is supposed to weed the garden. He wants Dad to show him which plants are weeds and which are not.

____ 4. Joanie cleans the bathroom without being asked, but usually misses something.

____ 5. Kim agreed to clean her room, but she needs constant help to avoid getting distracted.

____ 6. Steve has kept his room clean since it was repainted.

Possible answers:

1. Needs supervision	2. Works independently	3. Needs assistance
4. Needs supervision	5. Needs assistance	6. Works independently

chance to dress himself. In other cases, parents tell their children what they expect or fear. For example, "When you are a little older you will be able to clean the bathroom by yourself." Or, "Careful where you roughhouse. Next thing I know, you will break a lamp." In Chapter 2, we will look at how our language affects responsibility.

How responsible are you?

Children learn more from what we do than what we say. If you wish to help a child become more responsible, look at the models provided by the adults in his or her life.

Most people are responsible in areas that are important to them. However, there are usually areas where they are not responsible. Here are several examples: the woman who prepares elaborate budgets for work and yet does not balance her checkbook; the man who manages many small details of several projects at one time, and often forgets his keys; or the tired parent who promises to read a story "later," but "later" never comes. You can review areas where you are responsible in Exercise 1-3: How Responsible Are You?

Children often pick up parents' attitudes toward responsibility. Parents often put children off with unfulfilled promises. "Let me finish this now, and I'll play with you later," or "I can't go to the park today, but we can go next week." In spite of good intentions, "later" and "next week" never come. These parents may have reasonable explanations, at least in their own minds, but the fact is they were not dependable. Many children conclude that

```
┌─────────────────────────────────────────────────────────────────────────┐
│                 EXERCISE 1-3:  How Responsible Are You?                   │
│                                                                           │
│  Instructions:  Read the list of activities below. Check how often you    │
│  do them.                                                                 │
│        A = Always, U = Usually, S = Sometimes, N = Never                  │
│                                                                           │
│  ____  1. Arrive on time to church or meetings    ____  6. Forget to mail │
│  ____  2. Write checks without enough money           letters             │
│         to cover them                             ____  7. Make your bed  │
│  ____  3. Complete tasks (projects) on time            in the morning     │
│  ____  4. Travel 65 miles per hour in a 55 mph    ____  8. Let the grass  │
│         zone                                           grow another week  │
│  ____  5. Remember to put away all your clothes   ____  9. Pay bills      │
│                                                        promptly           │
│                                                   ____ 10. Watch TV (or   │
│                                                        read) instead of   │
│                                                        doing tasks        │
└─────────────────────────────────────────────────────────────────────────┘
```

Possible answers: The odd numbered items are usually considered responsible behaviors and the even numbered items are frequently considered irresponsible.

"promises" are made to be broken. Later, these same parents wonder why their children do not clean their rooms or take out the trash.

Needs of school-aged children

Children need positive self-esteem, reasonable limits, and the opportunity and expectation for growth. We will look briefly at each of these and how they affect the development of responsibility.

Self-esteem. All children need to feel good about themselves. A positive self-image comes from feeling lovable and capable. Children create their self-images from the messages they receive about themselves, their experiences, and the decisions they make about those experiences and messages. Children who believe they are capable, responsible people find it easier to learn a task.

Reasonable limits. Reasonable limits give children a sense of security and a direction for movement. In general, the particular set of rules a family lives by seems less important than having clear and consistent rules. Clear, healthy rules permit children to grow within many different value systems. However, some families have unhealthy rules, such as to ignore heavy drinking or incest. Unhealthy rules, even unspoken, need to be acknowledged and changed.

Opportunity for growth. Children do not magically become responsible on their sixteenth birthdays or when they leave home. It is a process that happens gradually over many years. Children who are given many opportunities to be responsible and are expected to act responsibly will find it easier to develop responsibility.

When my older sister, Roberta, was sixteen, she wanted an allowance to buy clothes. She had never managed money before, but she convinced Mom and Dad to give her six months allowance so she could take advantage of the back-to-school sales to buy school clothes. She blew all the money in the first three weeks.

Later, when my youngest sister, Becky, was twelve, she also began to pester my parents for a six month clothing allowance. This time my parents substituted a monthly clothing allowance. Becky quickly learned to save her money for more expensive purchases. Two years later she went to a quarterly allowance, and in two years more she went to a six month allowance with no trouble.

Children need opportunities to grow, but the opportunities need to be related to both their ages and their experience levels.

Developmental tasks of children

Several different approaches to developmental tasks exist. One approach I find useful is the recycling theory presented in Jean Illsley Clarke's book, *Self-Esteem: A Family Affair*. In this approach, each age has a particular task children focus on. However, children may also be recycling, or working on, previous tasks as well.

When you are looking at what is reasonable to expect of children, it is helpful to look at what developmental tasks they are working on. A four-year-old who is experimenting with power may refuse to cooperate simply to see how *you* use power. A ten-year-old may be more interested in how his neighbors make beds and set the table than how his family does.

As people pass through each stage of development, they often return and work on a previous level in a new way. This is why a six-year-old who is starting a new level of development may need extra loving, care, and support; or why an eight-year-old who is saying "no" (like a two-year-old) needs clear, firm limits and support. Parents often recycle the same issues their children are working on. This makes family life particularly challenging when both parents and children are recycling power issues or saying "no."

Can I mow the lawn yet? Pick Up Your Socks

Developmental Tasks

Age	Children's Tasks	Parents' Tasks
0-6 months	**Being:** To decide to live and grow.	Nurture, love, care, and support babies.
6-18 months	**Exploring:** To explore their world.	Provide a safe environment for toddlers to explore.
18-36 months	**Thinking:** To begin to think and to distinguish between thinking and feeling. To separate from their parents.	Encourage thinking, distinguish between feelings and behavior, and accept children's feelings. Recognize "No's" as the beginning of separation rather than as disobedience.
3-6 years	**Power:** To observe how people (both men and women) get what they want and decide how to use power.	Model appropriate use of power. Establish consequences for misuse of power. Accept children's need to test limits without feeling personally threatened.
6-12 years	**Structure:** To find out how the world works and to develop a structure for living in it.	Offer skills and support to children as they develop rules for living with their peers and family. Particularly help them make decisions and motivate *themselves* to follow through.
12-18 years	**Sexuality:** To decide who they are as males or females. To continue to separate from their parents.	Gradually turn over decision making to teens. Help them discover the consequences of their decisions.

What is reasonable for your child?

Children are different. What is reasonable to expect for one child may be totally unrealistic for another. Further, parents differ in what they want for their children. To determine what is reasonable for your children, begin by looking at your values, then consider each child's age, temperament, experience, and learning style.

Identify your goals. Sometimes parents feel discontented with a child without understanding why. One way to focus on your desires is to look at your values. You can think in terms of either what you want now, or what you want for your child at twelve or eighteen years of age. It is helpful to record your goals so you can see them develop or revise them if needed. Exercise 1-4: Identifying Values For Children will help you focus on your own goals for them.

Consider age. Few people expect the same behavior from a four-year-old, an eight-year-old, and a twelve-year-old. If you are concerned about a particular issue, check with parents of children your child's age to find out what their children do. A chart of household jobs children do at different ages is presented in Chapter 4.

EXERCISE 1-4: Identifying Values For Children

Instructions: Imagine you are about to adopt a child and you find that child has the following characteristics. Mark how you would feel about each statement.

H=Horrified, **C**=Concerned, **N**=Neutral, **P**=Pleased, **E**=Elated

H	C	N	P	E	Your adopted child —
[ ]	[ ]	[ ]	[ ]	[ ]	1. is very active, always on the go and moving.
[ ]	[ ]	[ ]	[ ]	[ ]	2. goes directly for whatever he or she wants.
[ ]	[ ]	[ ]	[ ]	[ ]	3. can catch and throw a ball very well.
[ ]	[ ]	[ ]	[ ]	[ ]	4. is a very attractive child.
[ ]	[ ]	[ ]	[ ]	[ ]	5. always greets people cheerfully.
[ ]	[ ]	[ ]	[ ]	[ ]	6. wants to wear only fresh, clean clothes.
[ ]	[ ]	[ ]	[ ]	[ ]	7. can do physical things easily (e.g., bike, jump rope, hit a ball).
[ ]	[ ]	[ ]	[ ]	[ ]	8. faces unpleasant situations (e.g., dentist, defending someone against a bully) without flinching.
[ ]	[ ]	[ ]	[ ]	[ ]	9. asks questions about everything.
[ ]	[ ]	[ ]	[ ]	[ ]	10. can do things a variety of ways.
[ ]	[ ]	[ ]	[ ]	[ ]	11. always replaces caps on felt-tip pens.
[ ]	[ ]	[ ]	[ ]	[ ]	12. lends money and possessions to anyone who asks.
[ ]	[ ]	[ ]	[ ]	[ ]	13. sees what needs to be done and helps without expecting a reward.
[ ]	[ ]	[ ]	[ ]	[ ]	14. tells the truth even when it is to his or her disadvantage.
[ ]	[ ]	[ ]	[ ]	[ ]	15. always wants to do things by himself or herself (e.g., walk to the store, build the camp fire).
[ ]	[ ]	[ ]	[ ]	[ ]	16. is tested as academically gifted.
[ ]	[ ]	[ ]	[ ]	[ ]	17. does what he or she is told without questions.
[ ]	[ ]	[ ]	[ ]	[ ]	18. lets other children "cut in line" without protesting.
[ ]	[ ]	[ ]	[ ]	[ ]	19. doesn't like activities interrupted.
[ ]	[ ]	[ ]	[ ]	[ ]	20. always thanks people.
[ ]	[ ]	[ ]	[ ]	[ ]	21. is always sought out by peers.
[ ]	[ ]	[ ]	[ ]	[ ]	22. says prayers every night without reminding.
[ ]	[ ]	[ ]	[ ]	[ ]	23. can be trusted to leave tempting items alone.
[ ]	[ ]	[ ]	[ ]	[ ]	24. befriends the new or unpopular child.
[ ]	[ ]	[ ]	[ ]	[ ]	25. gets own snack whenever hungry.

Values these examples are intended to illustrate are on the following page.

Parents' expectations are not always in line with children's abilities. This can be seen in the following table by examining how the common complaints about children's behavior vary with their age.

Temperament differences. Research suggests that children are born with a basic temperament. The basic temperament can be modified, but not changed completely. Doctors Chess, Thomas, and Birch, in their book *Your Child is a Person*, identify nine traits that remain relatively consistent. These are activity level, persistence, intensity of response, regularity, adaptability, physical sensitivity, distractibility, positive or negative mood, and reaction to new situations.

The two traits that most directly affect responsibility are distractibility and persistence. Children differ in persistence. Some give up quickly, others go on and on. If a child can stick to tasks of her choice for hours, you can teach her to transfer that persistence to other areas. If a child does not persist at tasks, you can teach her persistence directly. Similarly, a child who is easily distracted may have difficulty remembering to return to the task.

Experience. A child's or teen's degree of responsibility is affected by what he or she has done. Successful experience provides both *factual information* (like how to clean the bathroom, the sum of seven plus eight, or ways to entertain a younger sibling) and *process information* (how to start something, how and when to get help, and how to keep going until it's done). If a child knows how to entertain and care for his brother and sister, it will be easier for him to babysit for other children. Even unsuccessful experiences can be helpful if children are taught to look at what happened and decide how they can do better.

Different learning styles. Each person has his or her own learning style. Children's learning styles are often different from their parents'. If you are married, your learning style is probably different from your spouse's.

The three most common ways to collect information are seeing, listening, and doing. Rita Dunn, of the Center for the Study of Learning and Teaching Styles at St. John's University, indicates that learning styles appear gradually. Most kindergarteners are *kinesthetic*. Children begin to develop *visual* strengths about third or fourth grade, and *auditory* skills around fifth or sixth grade.

Some people become effective with all three styles; however, other people develop a single preferred mode. Visual learners will remember 75% of what

---

Examples on the preceding page were intended to illustrate the following traits:

1. Active, full of energy; 2. Aggressive, competitive; 3. Athletic, does well in sports; 4. Attractive, physically nice looking; 5. Cheerful, pleasant; 6. Clean, neat; 7. Coordinated, physically able; 8. Courageous, stands up for own beliefs; 9. Curious, inquisitive; 10. Flexible, resourceful; 11. Frugal, conserves resources; 12. Generous, shares with others; 13. Helpful to others, altruistic; 14. Honest, truthful; 15. Independent, self-reliant; 16. Intelligent, intellectual; 17. Obedient, compliant; 18. Passive, yielding; 19. Persistent, has "finishing power"; 20. Polite, well mannered; 21. Popular, liked by peers; 22. Religious, respects God; 23. Self-controlled, self-restrained; 24. Sensitive, considerate of others's feelings; 25. Independent, takes care of self.

Chart 1-1: Common Concerns at Different Ages Behaviors listed in decreasing frequency and reported by at least one third of the parents responding. Starred (*) behaviors reported by at least half the parents.

3-Year-Old
*Interrupts when I'm on the phone
*Whines
*Interrupts when I talk to people
*Hits
Cries
Ignores what I say
Trouble going to bed
Talks back
Teases
Temper tantrums
Doesn't share

4-Year-Old
*Interrupts when I talk to people
*Whines
*Interrupts when I'm on the phone
*Ignores what I say
Hits
Dawdles
Talks back
Cries
Doesn't clean room
Doesn't share
Temper tantrums
Teases
Doesn't do chores
Trouble going to bed
Name calling
Tattles
Bathroom language

5-Year-Old
*Interrupts when I talk to people
*Interrupts when I'm on the phone
*Whines
*Doesn't do chores
Doesn't clean room
Ignores what I say
Teases
Talks back
Tattles
Dawdles
Trouble going to bed
Cries
Hits

6-Year-Old
*Interrupts when I'm on the phone
*Interrupts when I talk to people
*Ignores what I say
*Teases
*Doesn't clean room
Doesn't do chores
Hits
Trouble going to bed
Talks back
Dawdles
Whines
Name calling
Tattles

7-Year-Old
*Doesn't do chores
*Dawdles
Interrupts when I'm on the phone
Interrupts when I talk to people
Doesn't clean room
Tattles
Ignores what I say
Teases
Trouble going to bed
Talks back
Moody

8-Year-Old
*Doesn't clean room
*Doesn't do chores
*Dawdles
Teases
Interrupts when I'm on the phone
Doesn't brush teeth
Talks back
Ignores what I say
Lies
Interrupts when I talk to people
Cries
Trouble going to bed

9-Year-Old
*Doesn't brush teeth
*Teases
*Doesn't do chores
*Doesn't clean room
*Interrupts when I'm on the phone
*Interrupts when I talk to people
Talks back
Lies
Tattles
Moody
Whines
Name calling
Ignores what I say
Dawdles
Hits

10-Year-Old
*Doesn't do chores
*Doesn't clean room
*Teases
Dawdles
Talks back
Interrupts when I'm on the phone
Interrupts when I talk to people

11-Year-Old
*Talks back
*Teases
*Doesn't do chores
*Doesn't clean room
*Name calling
*Ignores what I say
*Doesn't brush teeth
Moody
Hits
Interrupts when I'm on the phone
Dawdles

12-Year-Old
*Talks back
*Doesn't do chores
*Doesn't clean room
*Teases
*Doesn't brush teeth
*Ignores what I say
Hits
Lies
Dawdles
Low grades
Name calling
Moody
Trouble going to bed
Interrupts when I'm on the phone

13-Year-Old
*Teases
*Doesn't clean room
*Doesn't do chores
*Trouble getting up
*Ignores what I say
*Name calling
*Moody
Doesn't brush teeth
Talks back
Dawdles
Lies
Low grades
Hits
Trouble going to bed
Tattles

14-Year-Old
*Ignores what I say
Doesn't do chores
Teases
Trouble going to bed
Moody
Talks back
Doesn't share
Doesn't clean room
Doesn't brush teeth
Disruptive in class
Trouble getting up
Name calling

Summary of Learning Differences

	Kinesthetic	Auditory	Visual
Learning Style	Learns by doing; direct involvement.	Learns through verbal instruction, either from others or self.	Learns by seeing; watches demonstrations.
Memory	Remembers best what was done, seen, or talked about. May take notes and not look at them.	Remembers names, forgets faces; remembers by auditory repetition.	Remembers faces, forgets names; writes things down. Takes notes and looks at them.
Problem Solving	Attacks problem physically; impulsive; often selects solutions involving greatest activity.	Talks problems out; tries solutions verbally, subvocally; talks self through problem.	Deliberate; plans in advance; organizes thoughts by writing them; lists problems.
Communication	Gestures when speaking; does not listen well; stands close while speaking or listening.	Enjoys listening but cannot wait to talk; descriptions are long and repetitive.	Quiet; does not talk at length; becomes impatient when extensive listening is required.
Language	Uses words such as *get, take, make,* etc.	Uses words such as *listen, hear, tell,* etc.	Uses words such as *see, look, watch,* etc.

they see in a 40 minute class period. An auditory learner will remember 75% of what he or she hears. Parents will be more successful communicating with their child if they use the child's preferred mode of learning. One parent described this as follows.

My kids are very different. It took me a long time to realize how different they were. Not only were they different ages and personalities, but they understood differently. Mary Beth is very visual. When I talked to her it was like talking to the wind. Nothing! Then it hit me that the times I had success with getting her to do things were times I left her a note as a reminder. Further, when she does something well, she appreciates a note more than my saying she did a neat job.

With my son John, it is just the opposite. He works much better if I tell him what I want. When I leave him a note, he doesn't notice it. He will leave a note unread for days.

A brief description of the three modes of learning is presented above. You might like to check the different ways people in your family respond.

More information about learning styles and how to help children learn is presented in Chapter 5 on Schoolwork.

As you work with children, remember to build on what is already there. If you want to remind an auditory child, telling him is fine. If you want to remind a visual child, write a note or keep your verbal messages very short. Exercise 1-5 will help you practice adapting to children's learning styles.

Summary In this chapter we have looked at what responsibility is, some children's needs, how children differ, and differences in what parents want for their children. When you have an idea of what you want and what your child is like, you are in the position to build on what is there. In the next chapter, we will look at some specific things adults can do to encourage responsible behavior.

Additional Reading

Self-Esteem: A Family Affair by Jean Illsley Clarke. Harper & Row, New York, 1978.

Know Your Child: An Authoritative Guide for Today's Parents by Stella Chess and Alexander Thomas. Basic Book Inc., New York, 1987.

"A Learning Style Primer" by Rita Dunn. *Principal*, May 1981, pages 31-34.

CHAPTER 2: BUILDING SKILLS

Responsibility does not magically appear at 12 years of age or 18 or 21. It develops over time. Like learning to walk, some children discover responsibility on their own. Others need to be taught the skills they need to be responsible. In this chapter, we will look at some of those skills and what you can do to help children learn them. In particular, we will consider decision making, problem solving, memory, and motivational skills.

Decision-making ability

Much of a person's ability to act responsibly depends on his or her ability to make decisions. This process begins with making simple choices as a toddler, talking about consequences, and progresses to problem solving as a child grows.

Offer choices. Decision-making ability begins with simple either/or choices. You can offer preschoolers the choice, "Do you want to walk to bed or be carried to bed?" If the child runs from the room, the parent can pick the child up and say, "I see you choose to be carried to bed." As the child becomes familiar with simple choices, you can add more alternatives.

The more ideas a child considers, the more likely he or she will be to choose something appropriate. You can help children by offering them several choices at one time. For example, "It's cold out. Do you want to wear your red sweater, your blue sweater, or your jacket?" If the child refuses to select one, you can offer the simple choice, "Do you want to decide what to wear, or shall I?"

Ask for options. When children can understand several alternatives, begin to ask them what they have considered. This helps children begin the process of thinking of alternatives for themselves. This is illustrated in the example below.

Melissa knew what she wanted. She wanted to ride the bike her cousin, Stacy, was using. When Stacy refused to get off, Melissa started to pull her off. Dad intervened by saying, "I cannot let you hurt Stacy. She will give you the bike when she is done. What can you do while you wait?"
"Nothing."
Dad replied, "You could do nothing. What else can you think of doing?" At that point Melissa mentioned several ideas and occupied herself happily until the bike was free.

Talk about possible consequences. Children need to know that behavior has consequences, and that different behaviors may have different consequences. "What might happen if you threw something at the boy who is teasing you?" "What might happen if you suddenly leaned way out of a canoe to grab the suntan lotion you dropped?" "What do you think will happen if you do not set the table?"

You can talk about consequences ahead of time, at the time the event occurs, or later. The purpose of the discussion is to *help children think* about a situation, not to tell them what they should do.

Teach children to solve problems

Effective problem solving has several parts: defining the problem; collecting data; looking at options; and making a decision. The problem may be as simple as setting the table or as complex as "staying out of trouble."

Define the problem. First, look at the situation and what the children want to happen. Then, state the problem in terms of all people involved.

Gather data. When does the problem occur? Who is affected? Who can help? Is time critical?

Consider many options. Encourage the children to collect as many ideas as they can—both practical and not so practical. Many people find when they list the ideas, they can think of only five or six. Those ideas are usually the ones they already knew. Add some silly ideas. When your mind is free enough to think of new, silly ideas, it is free enough to think of new, good ideas. Go for at least a dozen ideas. If you need more, you can get some from other people.

Evaluate ideas and make a choice. Remind children to review each of the options. Is it reasonable? Is it something you can follow through with? Is it respectful to all people involved? Is it agreeable to all people it will affect?

Plan, implement, and evaluate. Remember, people are more likely to support a decision they helped make. Plan a time to evaluate. Most plans need revisions. If the plan has trouble, revise it and try again. If the plan works well, congratulate yourself, and remember what you did.

The process of problem solving works both for adults and children. It can be used both to teach children to resolve problems themselves and to modify children's behavior. Here is an example of how one child used it.

Annie and a friend bought a mouse to keep at school. Since none of their parents would let them bring it home, Annie arranged for another friend, Danny, to take it home for winter vacation. Danny's parents agreed, and all was fine...until Danny's bus driver refused to let him take the mouse on the bus.

Problem: *What to do with the mouse for vacation?*

Gather data: *Annie knew she had to decide what to do fast. Half the buses had left. It would take at least five minutes to walk to the school office to phone home. If she did that, she would miss her bus.*

Options: *(1) See if someone on another bus could take the mouse home. (2) Leave the mouse and cage on the sidewalk. (3) Run to the office and try to phone home for permission to bring the mouse home. (4) Take the mouse on her bus and hope her parents would let her keep it. (5) Take it home, and have her parents take the mouse to Danny's. (6) Call home and ask to be picked up and driven to Danny's house to deliver the mouse.*

Make a decision: *Annie decided to first see if someone else could take the mouse home. If not, she would take it home herself, since her mom might not* *be home yet. If she tried to phone, she might miss the bus and be stuck at school. When she got home, she would explain the situation and hope her parents wouldn't get too mad.*

Plan, implement, and evaluate: *Annie took the mouse home. As she walked in, she said, "Mom, I know I'm not supposed to bring the mouse home, but Danny's bus driver wouldn't let it on the bus. If I can't keep it, we can phone and see if Danny can still have it. If I phoned to ask you, the bus would have left." Her mom was not happy, but thought Annie did her best under the circumstances.*

This same process can be used to resolve conflicts between children, and problems between adults and children. When you facilitate a conflict between two children, act impartially. If you have a particular solution you want the children to choose, talk with them directly about that alternative rather than helping them resolve their problem. If you wish to negotiate with a child, remember to listen to the child's concerns and ideas openly. If you have preconceived ideas about how the negotiations should go, you will probably miss the opportunity for new, good ideas. You can practice this process in Exercise 2-1.

Collecting information and making decisions is a large part of the process of responsibility. However, unless children can remember their plans and motivate themselves to finish them, their intentions do them no good.

Teach memory skills

How many times have you heard the excuse, "I forgot"? Many people, both children and adults, want to do things, but forget. They are not necessarily lazy or thoughtless. They may simply need to learn ways to remember things. This section will briefly look at how memory works, and then look at some specific ways children can remember responsibilities.

Three steps for remembering something are *recording* the information, filing or *retaining* it in your mind, and *retrieving* it. Often when people say they forgot something, the problem was that they never recorded or filed the information, and so it was not available for retrieval. In other cases, people may have recorded the information, but did not file it in a way they could find it easily later. The advantage of a well organized file (or memory) is illustrated below.

Suppose you went to a friend's house to borrow a book. If the books were all shelved in order (by author or title) you could find the book fairly easily. However, suppose all the books were dumped on the floor in one room. It would probably take you a long while to find the book.

Many memory aids provide a system to help you file information. Both children and adults can improve their memory by practicing recalling or retrieving the information they store.

Long vs. short term-memory. Memory consists of at least two different processes. These processes appear to be physically dissimilar in the brain. Short-term memory can hold up to seven pieces of information and is brief. Short-term recall is easy, and forgetting is very rapid. An example of short-

EXERCISE 2-1: Problem Solving Process

Instructions: Read the situation and follow the problem solving steps.

Situation: Matthew does not get up in time for school. You do not want to take him to school.

Problem:

Gather data:

List choices:

Decide what to do:

Plan, implement, and evaluate:

Possible Answer:

Define problem. Matthew has trouble getting up mornings in time for school.

Gather data. Does he have trouble every day (weekends as well as school days)? Is it related to staying up late at night? Is he having trouble at school with the kids, teacher, or material? This information may suggest a way to handle the problem.

List choices. Assuming he was not having physical problems or trouble at school, you might: get him an alarm clock; offer a special breakfast if he is up and dressed by a certain time; allow him one skip or absence a quarter that he can take when he wants; take a damp washcloth and wipe his face while he is in bed; let the family pet in to pester him; vacuum the hall by his room; open the curtains to let in lots of light; send him to bed earlier if he can't wake up; make a contract with him outlining benefits and consequences of waking up promptly; etc.

Make a decision. Talk with Matthew about what he thinks might help. Decision--get him an alarm clock and allow him one skip a quarter.

Plan, implement, & evaluate. Take Matthew to the store and let him choose an alarm. If he is in bed 10 minutes after the alarm, ask him if this is his skip for the quarter.

Pick Up Your Socks

term memory is looking up a phone number and then dialing it. If you are interrupted, you often will be unable to recall the number.

Long-term memory is relatively permanent and has an apparently unlimited storage capacity. Information from the short-term memory is coded in some way to enable it to be transferred to long-term memory. If the information is not coded and stored in an orderly fashion, it will be difficult to retrieve.

Memory aids associate the information to be remembered with something else more likely to be remembered. There are four steps in this process: picking a key word, choosing a helper, forming an association between task and helper, and practicing using the helper to remember the task. The process is illustrated in the following example.

Lindsey (age 12) had trouble remembering to floss and brush her teeth each evening. Although she was willing to brush, I did not like reminding her every time. After several failures we found an approach that worked—Lindsey would brush and floss in the shower. The shower was her helper. She associated the shower with brushing her teeth (she visualized the shower cleaning her teeth). For about a week we made up silly stories about strange showers. We would describe the conditions in great detail. Then Lindsey would mentally pretend to bathe in the strange showers and practice remembering to brush and floss her teeth.

Memory Association Process

Steps	Explanation	Example
Pick a *Key word*	Represents the task or information to be remembered	Cat—feed the cat
Choose a *Helper*	Something you will notice or remember later. For example: a person, place (kitchen), thing (string around your finger), or sound (buzzer ring).	Milk—from the carton he uses each morning
Make an *Association*	Form a connection—silly or logical—between the key word and the helper. For most people, silly, active associations are more powerful than static ones.	Cat taking a bath in the milk *or* pouring the milk on the cereal.
Practice	Imagine noticing the helper and associating it with the original task. The more detailed the images, the more effective the process.	First imagining (*or* drawing) pictures of the cat bathing in milk (or pouring milk on cereal). Then imagining getting up and feeding the cat.

Teaching children to motivate themselves involves switching from external to internal motivation, introducing long-term goals, dividing a task into small steps, and discussing ways for children to collect support.

Shift from external to internal motivation. You can begin to shift the responsibility for motivation to the child by offering both "external" and "internal" rewards and praise. For example, when a child finishes a task the parent can say, "I'm proud of you [external reward]. I bet you feel proud of yourself too [internal reward]." If a child is having trouble learning a task, you can set up positive expectations by saying, "Imagine how good you will feel to be able to set the table by yourself."

When you begin to switch to internal motivation, let your child become involved in selecting and thinking of rewards which will work for her. For example, "You want to play the flute. I would like to help you. Would it be more helpful if I played a game with you when you finish practicing or if you get a ticket? Remember, five tickets and we go to McDonalds™ for lunch." Another time, you might sit down together and list many ways you both could work together. Later you will be able to offer help without making specific suggestions. For example, "Sounds like you want to improve your math grade. Is there any way I can help you?" This gives the child the clear message, "You are responsible, and I am available to help."

Praise and rewards from others are nice; however, if children are to act responsibly, they need to develop the ability to motivate themselves. When children begin to feel responsible, they usually need less external help because they have developed some skills for getting themselves started. This is particularly true if they are working toward something important to them. You can practice shifting motivation from external to internal in Exercise 2-2.

Introduce long-term goals. Children need to learn to plan and carry out long-range plans. The distance and complexity of the goal will depend on the child's age and experience. For example, a goal for a seven-year-old might be to learn to ride a bike well enough to participate in the bike rodeo in the fall. A goal for a 12-year-old might be to save enough money for a new bike before summer.

Effective goals are specific. They specify both a measurable *criterion* for success and a *date* for completion. For example, both "to improve my spelling," and "to learn to ride a horse this year" are unclear. What does "learn" mean? How much improvement is enough? When, during "this year," will the goal be completed?

When a goal is clear, anyone can decide if the person has completed it. For example, "I will increase my spelling grade from a C to a B by the end of the second quarter this year," or "I will reduce the number of spelling errors per 100 words from 20 to 10 by May 21st," are clear and objective. A note for parents: you may have goals for your child, but these are not your child's goals unless he or she *willingly* accepts them. However, even when children set their own goals, no matter how clear, few are successful without some assistance. You can practice identifying effective goals in Exercise 2-3.

Believe in the goal. Sometimes a child may want something but does not think it is possible to get it. You can help identify why the goal seems

EXERCISE 2-2: Shifting Motivation

Instructions: Each of these sentences relies on external motivation. Rewrite them so they also encourage the child to value himself or herself.

1. Ilana, I'm proud of you. You scored three goals today.

   _____

2. Harry, you cleaned your room all by yourself. I am delighted.

   _____

3. Jennifer, you got four A's. I am very pleased.

   _____

Possible answers: **1.** Ilana, you scored three goals today. I bet you're pleased with yourself. **2.** Harry, you can be proud of cleaning your whole room by yourself. **3.** You got four A's. I can see you're delighted.

EXERCISE 2-3: Identifying Effective Goals

Instructions: Read each goal. Mark it with a **C**, if the goal is clear and complete. Mark it with an **I**, if it is incomplete; then identify the error and suggest a change.

1. To reduce my freestyle time for swim team.

2. To earn $250 to buy a new bike.

3. To put my clothes away each night before I go to bed for one week, ending Sunday, April 24th.

4. To make the baseball team next Spring.

5. To earn enough money to buy a computer by March 10.

Possible answers:
1. Incomplete. Needs criteria and date. Better: Decrease swimming time by 10 seconds by the first swim meet. **2.** Incomplete. Needs date. **3.** Effective. **4.** Effective. Will probably need to make sub goals. **5.** Incomplete. Needs amount of money.

impossible for her, and help her develop a plan to succeed. For example, a child might think he cannot learn math because he is not smart enough. If that is the reason, an adult can help by finding ways to bolster his self-esteem in general and in math in particular. Perhaps the child needs to learn ways to memorize information. For many goals, dividing the task into small pieces makes it more achievable and believable.

Divide task into small steps. One way you can help children become responsible is to divide a long-term goal or complex task into small pieces and celebrate the completion of each step. As a child finishes one piece of the task, it becomes easier to do the next.

Zack, age eight, wanted a gerbil. His parents weren't crazy about the idea, but decided to use it as a learning opportunity. They said he could buy one if he saved the money. They took Zack to the pet store to price the cage, water bottle, food, and pet. The total, with tax, came to $37.31.

He got $1.00 a week allowance and 50 cents extra for chores. At that rate, it would take him about six months to save the money. That was longer than Zack could imagine waiting. However, his dad helped him make a plan.

It would take 17 weeks. Zack would get paid an additional 75 cents for doing some extra chores, and he would buy the things as he earned money for them. First he bought the feed ($1.35), next the water bottle ($2.64), then the cage, and, finally, the gerbil. Zack kept all the pet stuff in his room where he could see it. Purchasing the pieces helped Zack feel he was making progress even though it took a long time.

The key to the success of a plan will often be setting goals the child can see and believe in. Dividing tasks into small pieces is a skill that comes from practice. Two general approaches exist. One approach is to *start at the beginning*—take the whole task and divide it into smaller pieces. The second way it to *start at the end*—decide what is possible, and build up from there. This is illustrated in the example that follows.

Terri wanted to "get an A in Math." However, that goal seemed impossible to her. Her mom helped her develop a plan. They began by focusing on her homework. She received assignments four nights a week. The first step was to get an A on one homework paper. Second was to get

Help kids learn to plan.   Pick Up Your Socks

EXERCISE 2-4: Dividing Big Tasks

Instructions: Read each of the situations below and suggest two ways to divide the work—top-down (starting at the beginning), and bottom-up (starting at the bottom).

Situation 1: Cleaning a very messy room.

Top-down:

Bottom-up:

Situation 2: Learning to type from a typing book.

Top-down:

Bottom-up:

Possible answers:

Situation 1: Top-down: Divide room into several parts (bed, top two toy shelves, lower two shelves, half of the floor by the window, half the floor by the door) and take one part a day. Bottom-up: Work hard for 5 or 10 minutes each day, and clean what you can.

Situation 2: Top-down: Divide the number of lessons by the number of weeks in order to find the number of lessons per week. Reward self after 1st, 2nd, 5th, 10th, 15th, etc. lesson. Bottom-up: Practice for ten or fifteen minutes each day. Chart the hours practiced. Reward self after 30 minutes, 60 minutes, 2 hours, 4 hours, etc.

two A's in one week, third was to get three A's. When Terri got four A's in a week, she began to work for A's on seven out of eight days. By the time she was getting A's on seven of eight assignments, she began to believe an A in Math was possible for the report period. Her change of attitude was remarkable.

Dividing a task into small pieces makes it more manageable. You can practice breaking a task into small pieces in Exercise 2-4.

In some situations, parents may want to offer rewards to help get the child started. Once children begin to understand the process of dividing a task, ask them to suggest ways to break down a task. You might ask a child's help in dividing up a task of yours. They often like to use their skills to help their parents. If you continue to make plans for them, they will depend on you rather than learn to plan for themselves.

Collecting support. Children can use support to help motivate themselves in two ways. First, children can talk to people and ask them for help. Ways to help might be noticing when they are doing well, reminding them of what they want to do, or preventing them from doing things they don't want to do. Two examples are described below.

Beth, age 11, wanted to stop biting her nails. She decided to rub hand cream around her nails when she felt like biting them. She asked her family to bring her the hand cream when they saw her biting her nails. It took her about four months to stop, but it worked.

Robert wanted to buy a dirt bike. It cost $200. When he was discouraged, he would sometimes spend money he was saving on junk. He asked his mother to keep his money for him. He gave her the money as he earned it. Each week she would bring it out so he could count it; however, it wasn't around to tempt him.

Another way to get support is to *make a commitment to someone* that you will do something. Often, people have the strength to do something for, or with, someone else that they cannot do alone. This works with children also.

Jennifer was an active child, but she could not ride a bike. We thought that if we left her alone, she would get around to it. However, at age 10 she was still reluctant to ride a bike. At the beginning of the summer, her father and I decided it was time for her to learn.

My younger sister Kate (Jennifer's favorite aunt) told Jennifer she would take her on a two day bike trip at the end of the summer, if she learned to ride. Jennifer asked if Kate would help her learn. When Kate agreed, Jennifer said she would try. The commitment to her aunt kept her going when she wanted to stop.

Learning to motivate one's self is challenging. One way people learn about motivation and responsibility is through the language they hear.

Use responsible language

Language influences how we act and how we think. Messages that encourage high self-esteem also encourage responsibility. Jean Illsley Clarke, in *Self-Esteem: A Family Affair*, presents four styles of communicating. Each is characterized by different language or attitudes.

The four types of messages are: nurturing, structuring, criticizing, and marshmallowing. The first two types contribute toward self-esteem and responsibility. The second two hinder them. *Nurturing* messages tell people they are lovable and capable. *Structuring* messages give a person information on "how" to be successful or capable. *Criticizing* messages tell people they are failing or give information on how to fail. *Marshmallowing* messages tell people life is tough and they cannot be successful.

Marshmallowing messages are nurturing messages that have gone astray. They are intended to sound nice, but they invite the listener to fail. Likewise, critical messages are structuring messages gone astray. They give information on how to do poorly rather than how to be successful. The differences are shown in the responses below.

Pick Up Your Socks

-------- Four Types of Messages --------

Situation one: Janie has been invited to sleep overnight at a friend's house. She also wants to go to a horse show with her aunt on the same day. She asks her dad what she should do.

Nurturing	That's your decision, Janie. I know you will have fun whatever you decide to do. When you decide, let me know.
Structuring	There are several ways to decide. You could toss a coin, draw straws, or make a list of the pros and cons of each choice. If you want more ideas, let me know.
Criticizing	How should I know? If you would pay attention to what people say to you, things like this wouldn't happen.
Marshmallowing	That's hard. No matter what you do, someone will be unhappy.

Situation two: Mason has forgotten to take the trash out as he agreed. Mom wishes to remind him to do his job.

Nurturing	Mason, you can do better than this. Figure out a way to remember.
Structuring	Son, find a way to remind yourself to take out the trash. You can put a note on your door, tie a string on your finger, or something else. If these ideas don't work for you, tell me and we can think of more.
Criticizing	You've got to do better. Why can't you remember anything? Next thing I know you will forget to brush your teeth.
Marshmallowing	I wish you could remember to take the trash out. Oh well, I know you have many things on your mind.

Any information can be given positively. People often give marshmallowing messages intending to make a child feel good, but the messages don't have that result. Marshmallowing can often be corrected by visualizing the child as successful, then talking as though the child is growing and noticing what improvement has begun. You can use words like "growing," "learning," and "maturing." For example, "Why can't you put away your clothes?" becomes "I'm glad you hung up your new dress. Soon you'll toss your dirty clothes in the hamper, too."

Criticism is often intended to show children what they did wrong and motivate them to change, however it rarely works. Avoid words like "always" or "never" because they blind you to those times when a child is responsible. Children are not all bad, and if the good goes unnoticed, they often decide it is not worth continuing. Usually parents find it more successful to suggest ways the child could do better. If you have trouble thinking of more than two choices to offer, see the list of alternatives on the summary sheet in the appendix. You can practice rewording criticism in Exercise 2-5.

Trip words. Some common words invite children to stumble or fall in their development toward responsibility. These trip words deny a person's power and responsibility. Some phrases are "I forgot," "It was an accident," or "It wasn't my fault." They are used to excuse lack of responsibility. If

EXERCISE 2-5: Rewording Suggestions

Instructions: Read each situation. Identify what type of message it is and rewrite it more positively.

1. Paul, look at your spelling grade. It's no wonder you got such a low grade—you never study. If you keep this up, you'll be getting poor grades in math, too.

2. Annie, you forgot to change the cat litter again. Are you going to forget to feed the cat, too?

3. Franny, I like you, even if no one will play with you.

4. Chad, if I've told you once I've told you a thousand times, don't bounce the ball in the living room. Can't you see you might break a lamp?

5. (Looking at a D on the report card.) David, I guess there's nothing you can do if the teacher doesn't like you.

6. Eva, don't worry about not being picked for the team. Some people just aren't athletic. Other kids didn't make the team either.

Possible answers:
1. Critical. **Nurturing:** Paul, it looks like you are having trouble with spelling. You can improve your grade. Do you want to do it yourself or would you like some help?
2. Critical. **Nurturing:** Annie, you're smart. Figure out a way to remember to change the cat litter.
3. Marshmallowing. **Nurturing and structuring:** Franny, you are fun to be with. Figure out three ways to find someone to play with and tell me which you like best.
4. Critical. **Structuring:** Bounce the ball in the basement or outside. If you bounce the ball in the living room, I will take away the ball for a while.
5. Marshmallowing. **Structuring:** David, you can do better than a D. Talk to your teacher tomorrow and find out what the trouble is. Then decide what you need to do. On Thursday tell me your plan.
6. Marshmallowing. **Nurturing:** Eva, I love you whether you are on the team or not. You are smart. If you want to be on the team, you can figure out a way to get the skills you need.

Pick Up Your Socks

trip words are successful, they will be used more and more. Adults often encourage excuses with weak responses. Trip words can be countered by a strong response that requests a child to be responsible. Some examples are listed below.

-------- **Encourage Responsible Language** --------

Excuse	Weak Response	Strong Response
I forgot my homework assignment.	Well, okay. But don't let it happen again.	I'm sorry you forgot. Call someone and find out what the assignment is.
It wasn't my fault. She got too close.	I'm glad you didn't hurt her on purpose. Next time, be more careful where you swing the rope.	You are responsible for what your body does. If you hurt someone, you must do your best to make him or her feel good again.
It was an accident. I didn't mean to spill the milk.	I know you didn't mean to. I'll clean it up.	I know you didn't mean to. And you must watch what you do. Clean up the mess and pour yourself another glass.

Children collect information about how to act from what people say to them. Children can learn either how to be responsible or how to avoid taking responsibility.

Summary In this chapter we have looked at what children need to be responsible: decision making ability, problem solving skills, and the ability to remember and motivate themselves. We have also looked at how language affects responsibility. Some children pick up these skills easily. Others need to be taught deliberately. In the next chapter we will look at how to encourage desirable behavior, set reasonable limits, and develop effective consequences.

Additional Reading

Self-Esteem: A Family Affair by Jean Illsley Clarke. Harper & Row, New York, 1978.

Kids Can Cooperate: A Practical Guide to Teaching Problem Solving by Elizabeth Crary. Parenting Press, Inc., Seattle, Washington, 1984.

Your Memory: How It Works and How to Improve It by Kenneth L. Higbee, Ph.D. Prentice-Hall, Inc., Englewood Cliffs, New Jersey, 1977.

CHAPTER 3:   CHILD GUIDANCE IDEAS

Parents frequently ask, "How can I get my children to do what they should do?"   Most parents can list many things their child "should" do that he or she does *not* do.   One particular task adults have is to help children ages 6-12 develop their own internal discipline or structure.   Parents and teachers can encourage this by strengthening children's decision-making ability and gradually turning responsibility for the children's decisions over to them. Parents and teachers can also help children develop internal structure by encouraging desirable behavior with praise and reinforcement, and by providing children with clear, reasonable limits and permitting them to experience the consequences of their decisions.

Encouraging appropriate behavior

Most children learn more effectively when you encourage (or reward) desirable behavior rather than punish behavior you do not like.   When you praise desired behavior, you clearly communicate what you want.   When you punish undesirable behavior, children know what you dislike, but they may not know what you *do* want or *how* to do what you want.   The simplest form of encouragement is praise.

Praise can be simple or elaborate.   A simple "Thank you" or a smile when a child stops reading (or playing ball) to help you take in the groceries acknowledges his effort.   A more involved message is, "You did it.   You have been practicing math facts for two weeks, and you finally got an A in math." Some families use visual hand symbols such as "Okay" or sign language for "good" so they can communicate non-verbally.

Effective praise is specific.   Children are sometimes confused by general praise.   When a child comes bursting in from school and Mom says, "Good job," the child may not know if Mom is glad she closed the door, put away her books, or if Mom somehow heard she got a 100% on the Social Studies test.   "Wow, you cleaned your room all by yourself" or "I like the way you used color in that picture" give children clear ideas about what they did well.

Effective praise is immediate.   The closer praise comes to the desirable behavior, the more effective it will be.   You can even praise effort that the child is putting out without waiting for completion.   For example, "I like that. You are setting the table before I even ask."

Sometimes parents try to use praise of past events to change current behavior.   To many children, that comes across as a criticism of current behavior rather than appreciation of past effort. For example, when you say, "I really like how you cleaned your room last week," most kids will interpret it as, "I don't like your room this messy, why can't you keep it clean like last week?"

Effective praise is sincere. Sometimes parents want to praise, so they say something they think sounds nice. They may say something too general or something made up. Most children are aware when praise is not genuine. For example, "That is the nicest picture I have ever seen," could become "I like the way you used red and blue. I feel cheerful when I look at it." Or, "You look really pleased with the computer program you wrote."

Effective praise reflects a child's development. As children grow older, adults often need to change both the focus and the source of praise. First, the focus of praise needs to switch from the external to the internal. For example, "I am proud of you" can become "You can be proud of what you did." Second, parents need to be sensitive to whom the child wants praise from. Sometimes, during junior high and high school, children want praise from peers and outsiders rather than from their parents. If you can pass on kind words from someone else, children may appreciate them more. You can practice identifying effective praise in Exercise 3-1.

Praise works well when the behavior you want occurs occasionally; however adults sometimes need to provide more active encouragement. You can provide this encouragement by reinforcing desirable behavior in some concrete fashion.

Reinforcement systems

Children, and people in general, usually repeat activities that are enjoyable. You can encourage desired behavior by using a reinforcer. Reinforcers may be enjoyable in themselves or they may be associated with something enjoyable. Offering a suitable reward will help most children learn.

Factors affecting success of reinforcers. To be effective, the reward must be something the child wants or needs and given immediately after it is earned. The reward can be something quick—like a smile or praise—or it can be attention or something material.

When my son was little, we went through a stage where the best way to get him to do household tasks was to reward him with file cards. At that time his allowance was sufficient to keep him well stocked in file cards. However, these cards were special because they came from my desk. As soon as he completed a chore, I would give him a card.

Encourage independence. If you want excellence, reward excellence or effort toward it. If you want independence, reward it. An example of how one family rewarded independence follows.

We wanted our son Caleb to take the trash out himself. We paid him five cents if he took it out and replaced a bag in the waste paper basket when we asked. If he remembered to do it without asking, we paid him ten cents. We wanted to get him in the habit of taking the trash out regularly, and we wanted a bigger payoff for remembering it himself.

EXERCISE 3-1: Identifying Effective Praise

Instructions: Read each sentence. Decide if there is an error. If there is, identify the error and rephrase the statement effectively.

1. Tommy was playing checkers with his sister. Mom comes in and says, "Well done."

_____

2. "Gina, you did a great job of cleaning. Your floor is clear, your bed is tidy and all your clothes are put away."

_____

3. Rayona is watching TV. Mom comes in and says, "I forgot to tell you, but I like the way you started to study right after supper last Wednesday."

_____

4. After a soccer game, "Andrea, you are the best goalie in the state."

_____

5. "Gary, you cleaned up the bathroom well for a boy."

_____

Possible answers:
1. Unclear. *Better*: "Tommy, I'm glad you remembered to take out the trash." **2.** Effective.
3. Not immediate. *Better*: Tell her at the time. Now you could say "It is time to study."
4. Exaggerated (unless the player was chosen goalie of the year for their state). *Better*: "You played really well today. I was proud the way you blocked the last kick." **5.** Negative comparison, implies not really well done. *Better*: "Gary, you cleaned the bathroom well."

EXERCISE 3-2: Possible Rewards

Instructions: List rewards that might be of interest to your children.

_____ _____ _____

_____ _____ _____

Possible answers:
Stickers, privilege of having friends overnight, money, going to a hamburger stand for lunch, candy, stationery supplies, practicing ball with parent, trip to zoo, trip to a ball game.

Pick Up Your Socks

Some ideas. Parents have used many types of incentives. The following are just a few:

Praise — "Wow, you sure cleaned the bathroom fast. You must be proud of yourself."

Marble jar — All members of the family work together to fill the marble jar. If you do your job well when asked, you can put in a marble. If you do it well without reminding, you can put in two marbles. When the jar is full, the whole family goes out to eat (or some other family treat).

Tickets or points — are earned. Tickets are exchanged for items in "The Box." The box can have stationery supplies, inexpensive toys, or precious junk from garage sales or cereal boxes.

Privileges — When the child has done the task (e.g., setting the table) for seven days, he gets one day off or can stay up an hour later one night.

Mystery Cards — When the chore is done, the child may draw a mystery card. The card offers things like a hug, a treat (e.g., cookie or ice cream cone), attention (e.g., story or game), or a privilege. The child gets what is on the card she draws.

In Exercise 3-2 you can list rewards that your child likes or might like.

Set reasonable limits

Reasonable limits provide security for children as well as guidelines. Effective limits are clear, age-appropriate, and enforceable. Effective limits also present rules in a way that encourages safety and growth.

Clear limits. Limits are more effective if they are *specific and stated positively* rather than negatively. For example, "Don't leave your school things on the sofa" would permit a child to drop them on the floor or kitchen counter. "Hang up your coat and put your books in your room" is clearer.

Avoid questions like "Do you want to clean your room now?" unless you are willing to accept a "No." *Limit choices* when you want something done in a timely fashion. For example, "When are you going to clean your room?" could become "Clean your room by 2:00 so Alan can vacuum. Do you want to do it yourself or shall I help you?" Similarly, "Would you like to clean the bathroom now?" could become "You can go biking when the bathroom is clean." "Why don't you spread paper on the table before you paint?" implies that the child may choose to paint directly on the table. Instead the parent might say "Spread newspaper on the table before you start to paint. That way you won't damage the table and clean-up will be easier."

Age-appropriate. As children grow, the rules or limits should change. For example, you might limit a seven or eight-year-old child to riding her bike on the sidewalk. A nine or ten-year-old may be permitted to ride on the streets in your immediate neighborhood. An eleven or twelve-year-old might be allowed to ride to a friend's home farther away. Rules also need to reflect a child's experience. For example, if your child did not learn to ride a bike until ten, you may not want to let her ride out of your neighborhood at eleven.

Encourage self-esteem. Limits can provide protection and growth, or they can encourage hopelessness and despair. Jean Illsley Clarke, in *Growing*

Up Again, presents a continuum which contrasts several different limits. On one extreme, rigidity and criticism discourage children by automatically denying wants, needs, or ability. On the other end, indulgence and neglect discourage children by thoughtlessly agreeing to requests or ignoring demands. In the middle, negotiable and non-negotiable rules provide protection and freedom to grow and succeed. The differences are illustrated below.

Enforceable. Few parents can monitor what happens at school or a friend's home. Before you make a general rule, think about how you will monitor it and what you will do if the rule is broken. For example, parents who have restricted sweet snacks for preschoolers often find that when their

STRUCTURE CONTINUUM

Rigidity	Criticism	Non-negotiable Rule	Negotiable Rule	Indulgence	Neglect or Abandonment
Makes a rule then won't listen or change.	Adult belittles, exaggerates, negates as he/she enforces rule.	Listens and still enforces rule.	Listens and is willing to negotiate.	May listen, but does not enforce rule.	Doesn't care. Doesn't enforce rule.

Message for children

Rigidity	Criticism	Non-negotiable Rule	Negotiable Rule	Indulgence	Neglect or Abandonment
"Don't be. I cannot change my rule."	"Don't act responsibly. Here is how to fail."	"Your welfare and safety are important. I am in charge."	"Your needs are important. My needs are important. We can negotiate."	"Don't be responsible. I expect you to fail."	"Don't be. I don't care what happens to you."

Example: Requests for Money

Rigidity	Criticism	Non-negotiable Rule	Negotiable Rule	Indulgence	Neglect or Abandonment
"Don't ever ask for money. I will give you what you need."	"You are a spendthrift! You will only waste the money."	"Use your allowance wisely. No extra money is available."	"If you need more money, we can discuss ways for you to earn it."	"Here's some money. I can wait till next month to repair the car."	"Take what you want. I am gone, drunk, or too stressed out to respond."

Example: Use of the Bicycle

Rigidity	Criticism	Non-negotiable Rule	Negotiable Rule	Indulgence	Neglect or Abandonment
"Forget about the bike. I will tell you when you can ride it."	"You are careless. If you ride the bike, you will have an accident."	"You must obey the traffic laws and be back by 4:30." (Consequences known and enforced.)	"You may ride only in the neighborhood. If you want to go farther, we can talk about options."	"It's a long way to Paul's. If you have trouble I will come and get you."	"Go ahead. I don't care what you do."

Example: Family Rules about Smoking

Rigidity	Criticism	Non-negotiable Rule	Negotiable Rule	Indulgence	Neglect or Abandonment
"If you ever touch a cigarette, you are out of the family."	"You are always puffing—just like your aunt."	"You may not smoke while you live with us." (Consequences known and carried out.)	*No negotiable rule. Safety issues are not negotiable.*	"Smoking is not good for you, but one cigarette won't hurt."	"It's your life. I am absent, drunk, or too stressed out to respond."

Pick Up Your Socks

children are school-aged, they beg or trade friends for sweets. When you make rules you cannot or do not enforce, you teach children to ignore them.

When you make a rule that is unreasonable or ineffective, you can change it. You can practice identifying ineffective or unreasonable limits and correcting them in Exercise 3-3.

EXERCISE 3-3: Recognizing Effective Limits

Instructions: Read each situation. Identify the problem and write a more effective statement.

1. "Dinner is ready. When are you going to set the table?"

   Problem: _____

   More effective: _____

2. Parent tells latchkey child, "Take out the trash as soon as you get home from school each day."

   Problem: _____

   More effective: _____

3. To seven-year-old, "I want the whole bathroom clean in five minutes. Get busy."

   Problem: _____

   More effective: _____

4. "No, you can't go skiing with your friend. You'd break your leg or run over someone."

   Problem: _____

   More effective: _____

5. "You can't play outside until you clean up your stuff."

   Problem: _____

   More effective: _____

Possible answers:
1. Asking questions, need to make statement. "Dinner is almost ready. Come set the table now."
2. Not home to enforce. "Take the trash out before I get home. I will phone when I leave work."
3. Too big a job for most seven-year-old children to do in five minutes. Either "Company is coming, help me clean the bathroom now" or "Remember this is your month to clean the bathroom. If you need help, ask."
4. Critical, tells how to fail. Better, "You may go skiing with your friends after you have successfully completed level five of ski lessons."
5. Unclear what jobs must be done. Better, "You may play when your bed's made, clothes are put away, and the floor is clean."

No matter how reasonable your limits or how much fun you make jobs, anticipate that children will test them. Decide in advance what you will do. Children need to learn that the world at large is full of consequences. Forget to set your car brakes and turn your wheels on a hill, and your car will drift. Whether you are a grownup or a child, you will get burned if you touch a hot grill. These are both *natural consequences*—they require no intervention from other people. Using natural consequences for discipline is desirable whenever possible. However, sometimes natural consequences are too severe or irregular to be good learning tools. In those situations parents and teachers must devise logical consequences.

Logical consequences require adult intervention. Parents decide what will happen. For example, "If you break something, whether on purpose or by accident, you must do your best to fix it." "If you are bike riding and forget to return on time, you will be restricted to walking for two days."

There are two general types of logical consequences:

1. Withdraw a privilege for a short while if the privilege is misused (no television, bike, friends over, etc.).

2. Retribution. If damage is done, it must be repaired or undone as much as possible.

The purpose of consequences is learning, not punishment. There are many possible consequences for each behavior—finding one that works for you and your child takes time and usually gets easier with practice. Initially, you may want to tell your child, "I need to think about what I am going to do." Then leave the situation and take the time you need to develop an appropriate consequence for the child's behavior. Bonnie McCullough and Sue Monson, in *401 Ways to Get Your Kids to Work at Home,* offer these five questions as a guideline in choosing consequences:

Is the consequence reasonable? A reasonable consequence helps children learn, is fair, and is proportional to the offense. If children come late to dinner, it is reasonable that they eat cold food.

The consequence also needs to be reasonable in the context of your family. For example, if your daughter leaves an assignment or notebook at home, you may want to think twice about making a special trip to school. If your child helps you when you forget things, you may want to take the material to school to show your appreciation by helping her. However, if it is the third time this week your daughter has forgotten her homework, you may want to let her cope without it. You can help her get organized before she leaves by asking, "Do you have everything you need today?"

Sometimes when parents feel hurt or angry, they are tempted to say things, or make consequences, that are not reasonable. For example, it is not reasonable to sell a brand new bike that someone trips over, even if the child was warned to put it away. It would be more reasonable to impound the bike for a couple of days or a week, or have the child earn back the privilege of using the bike.

Is the consequence enforceable? Ask yourself, "Will this consequence cause me more work than I want?" Are you willing to leave a six-year-old, whose room is not clean, at home while you go to the zoo? If you say, "No snacks, since you didn't clean up," are you willing to stay home and watch the kitchen? Grounding your children for a week may punish *you*, particularly if your schedule is too full to help them find things to do. It is also unreasonable to create a consequence that will cause work for your spouse or day-care provider without getting his or her agreement first.

Is the consequence clearly related to the offense? When the consequence relates directly to the offense, it is more effective. For example, "No TV if you don't clean your plate" is not related, but "If you're not hungry enough for dinner, you're not hungry enough for dessert" is. Making children pay money to get clothes back they left lying in the family room may be related if you pay them for cleaning; however a more effective choice may be asking them to do a small job in exchange for the time involved in picking up.

Is the consequence consistent with nurturing care? The consequence needs to reflect the temperament and developmental needs of the child. For example, one woman wanted to reduce her sons' quarreling. Each time they argued she sent them to their separate rooms for an hour. This consequence did reduce the fighting between the boys, however they also stopped playing together. The consequences may need to be adjusted to the temperament or developmental level of the particular child. For example:

Melissa had just discovered friends. She had been so involved in books that other kids were unnecessary. I hoped her interest in people would encourage her to keep her room clean. I considered restricting friends' visits to times when her room was clean, because it is not safe to walk on a littered floor. This worked well with her older sister, but we decided that developmentally, Melissa needed friends more than she needed a clean room.

We decided to combine a consequence with a reward to help Melissa keep her room clean. We decided to spend 20 minutes each evening with Melissa. If her room was reasonably tidy, one of us would do whatever she wished. If the room was messy, we spent the time cleaning.

Is there anger, resentment, or retaliation associated with the consequence? Many times the anger a parent feels when he or she makes and enforces a consequence is conveyed to the child. As a result, the consequence may be unfair or presented in a critical manner. Another result is that the child feels as bad or as angry as the parent, and focuses on revenge rather than learning from the situation. For example, Mom throws out her son's favorite sweater because she is sick of picking it up from the living room floor, or Dad angrily increases the vacuuming job from the rec room to the whole house since the rec room was not clean on time as promised. When a parent acts angrily, much of the child's energy goes into warding off the anger or into mentally plotting revenge rather than focusing on how to do better next time. You can practice identifying effective consequences in Exercise 3-4.

EXERCISE 3-4: Identifying Consequences

Instructions: Read each sentence and decide if it is a good consequence using the five criteria. If not, identify the error and suggest a better consequence.

1. "If you don't bring the car back on time, you may not use it the next time you have something scheduled."

2. "Santa is not going to bring any new toys because you can't even clean up your old ones."

3. "You left the hammer outside to rust, so you must clean the rust off and oil the hammer."

4. "You can't have a friend over when your room is a mess (floor littered with stuff) because the friend might get hurt."

5. Parents, angry and embarrassed because their son had set off the fire alarm at school, told him, "You are a bad boy and don't deserve to have any toys." Then they took his toys out to the sidewalk and let children in the neighborhood take them.

6. Trash is to be taken out each day (before midnight). If not, the parent will wake the child up at 11:55 pm to take the trash out immediately.

Possible answers:
1. Good. **2.** Too harsh and not nurturing. Better to help child store or give away some toys, and then organize the rest. **3.** Good. **4.** Good. **5.** Too harsh and not related. Better to find out why the boy set off the alarm and deal with those issues. **6.** Reasonable if child is getting enough sleep.

Pick Up Your Socks

Make effective contracts

Contracts are used to clarify expectations and consequences. A contract is an agreement between two or more people. It is not a rule or requirement set by one person for another. If I say, "Tidy your room before I read to you," that is not a contract.

Uses of contracting. Contracts can focus on household jobs, practicing music, studying, or personal behavior. Contracts spell out the effort each party provides, the benefits each person receives, and the consequences to each for lack of compliance. A contract is appropriate when *both* parties agree to the goal. The contract outlines how they will work together. Three steps in making a contract are: clarify the purpose, decide who does what, and establish the benefits and consequences.

Clarify the purpose. Negotiate with the child and specify what is to be done, when and where. For example, does "clear the dinner table" mean just remove the dishes and silverware, or does it mean put away the leftovers, wipe the table, and sweep the floor? When will the table be cleared—immediately after dinner, brushing teeth, or anytime before bed time? Where are the dishes to be put—in the sink, on the counter, or rinsed and put in the dishwasher?

Further, how long will the contract run—a day, a week, a month? In general it is best to keep the initial contract short (a week or less) and then extend or revise it.

Decide who does what. Each person must be willing to provide some effort towards the goal and to accept the effort or input of the other person. For example, who is responsible for remembering to clear the dishes, and who makes sure there is a place in the kitchen for them? If Mom wishes to remind (nag) the child about the task, is the child willing to accept her effort? If not, Mom will need to think of another way to help.

Establish mutual consequences. There are benefits for keeping the contract, and penalties for breaking the contract. Create separate benefits and penalties for child and adult. The benefits can be a service, money, prestige, a privilege—whatever has meaning to the people involved.

The penalty can be loss of service or privilege for the offending person, or some amends to the injured party. When you establish consequences for failure to keep the contract, consider how they will be implemented. For example, you don't want to compound the situation of "not clearing the table" to "not clearing the table *and* not taking the trash out." If you contract for a kindness, find something the person is willing to do. It could be a treat (a batch of cookies, a picture, or a back rub) or a service (entertaining siblings, returning books to the library, or a simple repair). Jean Illsley Clarke, in *WE*, offers a structure for developing a contract. This approach was used to create a contract for the following example.

Ashley and her dad, Mike, both wanted Ashley to play the flute; however, Ashley frequently forgot to practice. After thinking about it, Dad decided he was willing for Ashley to give up the flute, if she really did not want to play. Ashley wanted to play the flute but didn't want her dad bugging her about it when she forgot. So they sat down and made the following contract.

Flute Practice Contract

Purpose: *Establish effective flute practice schedule/system.*

	Terms for Dad	**Terms for Ashley**
Service:	*Provide flute and lessons*	*Practice flute*
Place:	*- -*	*In the living room*
Hours:	*- -*	*30 minutes after school or before bedtime.*
Duration:	*One week*	*One week*
Benefit:	*Daughter who plays the flute.*	*Learns to play the flute.*
Mutual Effort	*Dad listens and helps only if Ashley asks. Dad may remind Ashley to practice only once a day. Ashley may say "Yes" or "No." Dad may not fuss or grump.*	*Ashley will practice 30 minutes on specified days (Monday, Tuesday, Wednesday, and Thursday) without reminding or complaining.*
Consequences	*Keeping the contract: Buy himself a new tape or record.*	*Keeping the contract: Go to ball game with Dad Friday night.*
	Breaking the contract: Not buy tape or record.	*Breaking the contract: Not go to ball game with Dad.*

Possible Answers for Rabbit Care Contract (Exercise 3-5)

Purpose: Establish rabbit care and family harmony

	Terms for Mom	**Terms for Nat**
Service:	Not nag Nat & supply rabbit food	Feed and water rabbit daily
Place:	--	Rabbit cage
Hours:	--	After school, before 4 pm
Duration:	One week	One week
Benefit:	Not to worry about the rabbit	To feel good about care of the rabbit
Mutual Effort:	Mom will supply rabbit food and check the rabbit at 3:50. If the rabbit has food and water, Mom will congratulate Nat. If not, she will remind Nat only once. If the rabbit is still not fed by 4 pm then Mom will do it.	Nat will care for the rabbit after school each day before 4 pm.
Consequences *Keeping the contract:*	Each day that Mom does her part she will treat herself to a half hour of recreational reading.	Each day that Nat cares for the rabbit he gets one ticket. When he collects five tickets, Mom will do the dishes for him one evening.
Breaking the contract:	If Mom reminds Nat more than once or fails to notice when Nat feeds the rabbit, Mom will do the dishes for Nat that evening.	Not go to ball game with Dad.

You can practice making a contract in Exercise 3-5. Making a contract is useful in many situations, however it is time consuming. In some situations parents and teachers need something that can be effective and lighten the tension. Humor can be an answer.

EXERCISE 3-5: Practice Contract

Instructions: Read the situation and prepare a contract.

Situation: Nat, age 10, loves animals. He is in charge of feeding and watering his rabbit, but he often forgets. Mom is willing to help him get in the habit of caring for it regularly. She is willing to do the dishes for him (a job which he hates).

Purpose: _____

	Terms for Parent	**Terms for Child**
Service:	_____	_____
	_____	_____
Place:	_____	_____
Hours:	_____	_____
Duration:	_____	_____
Benefit:	_____	_____
	_____	_____
Mutual Effort:	_____	_____
	_____	_____
	_____	_____
	_____	_____
Consequences:	*Keeping the contract:*	*Keeping the contract:*
	_____	_____
	_____	_____
	Breaking the contract:	*Breaking the contract:*
	_____	_____
	_____	_____

Utilize humor Humor is a powerful tool. When it is used appropriately it can build esteem, invite cooperation, and reduce tension. When used insensitively it can build resentment and decrease self-esteem. This is particularly true as children grow into teens. The question becomes how to introduce positive humor in your dealings with older children?

Focus on the incongruous. Effective humor for families focuses on the silly or incongruous. It takes the ordinary or expected and turns it around. It helps people view their actions in a new light, without demanding that they do so. This can be seen in the following example.

I can clearly remember when I discovered the benefits of humor as a guidance tool. My son, Ricky, was 14 and getting very feisty. He was standing beside the table and I reminded him it was his turn to set the table. He replied, "No!" and watched to see what I would do.

I was startled and angry and considered replying, "What do you mean 'No,' young man?" but I felt the situation might deteriorate. Instead I said, "I'm confused. Is that an 'I'll do it right now, "No,"' or an 'I'll do it in five minutes "No?"' He looked at me, laughed, and said "I'll do it now."

A side benefit of using humor for me was that, as soon as the idea popped into my head, I was no longer angry.

Speak from your perspective. Humor with others is more effective if it is offered from your point of view. If someone comes across as silly or confused, it should be you. Avoid comparing children negatively, even in a humorous way. One Dad's experience with his eleven-year-old follows.

One thing I hate is people clomping around the house. One morning, Rebecca was moving noisily down the hall. I called to her, "Rebecca, I have discovered a new way of moving. You pick one foot up, move it forward, and place it gently on the floor. Then you repeat the process with the other foot. I call it walking." She giggled and said, "Sorry, Dad, I guess I was a bit noisy."

This situation would not have been as effective if Dad had said, "Rebecca, I want you to try moving a new way." Even if the child does not change his or her behavior, you both will feel better for a laugh.

A laugh is worth a thousand nags.   Pick Up Your Socks

Use a normal voice tone and pattern. When you are using humor, give the impression that you are enjoying yourself. Keep your tone conversational and your choice of words and sentence construction normal. It is also important to speak clearly, so the child can hear every word. If children miss some of what you say, the humor may flop. As you use humor more often, you will develop your own style.

Picture children as changing

One of the simplest ways to help a child change is to see that child as changing. You can create an image of what you want in your mind.

Three elements. Shakti Gawain, in her book *Creative Visualization*, describes three elements necessary for effective visualization—desire, belief, and acceptance. First, you must truly want what you are visualizing, not passively ("it would be nice") but intensely. Second, you must believe that what you are visualizing is possible—possible when and where you want it. Third, you must be willing to accept the change that occurs. Sometimes parents are so wrapped up in the effort to change a child that they don't see the changes the child has made, or they reject the changes they see as not adequate.

Three steps. Visualization involves three steps. First, *relax* your body completely. Second, while you are relaxed, *picture the behavior you want* as clearly as possible. Imagine how you will feel, your child's feeling of success, and yourself congratulating the child and talking to others about how the change came about. Finally, *make some positive statement* (aloud or silently) that the desired behavior exists. One mother's experience with this process is described below.

Amy (age 10) came home from the first day of school almost hysterical. She got her name on the board and four check marks after it. Each mark meant she had done something wrong. I talked with her about what she had done and reviewed what I could do to help her. Nothing looked very hopeful. Although I had never used visualization for someone else, I decided to visualize her getting through the following day successfully.

Fortunately, my next day's work was simple paperwork. Every time I thought of Amy I would let go of my nervousness for her and relax. I mentally sent her love and support. I saw her stopping herself from getting in trouble, I saw her relaxing so she would not get nervous and do something wrong, and I imagined her surrounded by protective light. Then I told myself, "Congratulations, she made it."

I could tell when Amy came in that things were much better. She said she felt calmer even though the teacher was mean. She added that her friend, Sierra, reminded her several times so she didn't get her name on the board at all, although nine other kids did.

Some people ask, "If changing behavior is that easy and effective, why doesn't everybody do it?" The answer may be twofold—first, some people find it "different" and are unwilling to try new approaches; and second, some people find the active process of creating detailed images in the mind difficult.

Some hints. *Remember action begins with thought.* When we make something, we always begin with an idea. For example, when you make dinner, it begins with the idea, "I'll make dinner," or the thought, "I'm hungry."

Phrase affirmations in the present tense. "John is learning to set the table by himself," rather than "John will learn to set the table." Again, this acknowledges that change begins with thought before it is visible to others.

Express affirmation in a positive way. State what you *want*, rather than what you do not want. For example, change "Martin won't hit anyone at school today" to "Martin resolves problems constructively." Or change "Sally won't oversleep" to "Sally will awake on time and be refreshed."

Visualize ideas different ways. Some people are unable to make mental pictures. They visualize by mentally "talking about" or "thinking about" the ideas they want to create.

Summary

In this chapter we have looked at ways to encourage appropriate behavior, set reasonable limits, develop effective consequences, use humor, and visualize children as growing. Each of these techniques can be used in many ways. The challenge is to find ways that work for both you and your child. The next chapter offers some answers to that challenge because it will look at what jobs children do, how to introduce family jobs, and specific ways to encourage children to do them.

Additional Reading

Without Spanking or Spoiling: A Practical Approach to Toddler and Preschool Guidance by Elizabeth Crary. Parenting Press, Inc., Seattle, Washington, 1979.

Loving Your Child Is Not Enough: Positive Discipline That Works by Nancy Samalin and Martha M. Dablow. Penguin Books, New York, 1987.

How To Talk So Children Will Listen, and Listen So Children Will Talk by Adele Faber and Elaine Mazlish. Avon, New York, 1982.

401 Ways to Get Your Kids to Work at Home by Bonnie Runyan McCollough and Susan Walker Monson. St Martin's Press, New York, 1981.

Parent Effectiveness Training by Thomas Gordon. Peter H. Wyden, Publisher, New York, 1970.

Growing Up Again: Parenting Ourselves, Parenting Our Children by Jean Clarke and Connie Dawson. Harper/Hazelden, San Francisco, California, 1989.

"Contracts" by Jean Clark. *WE*: Newsletter for Nurturing Support Groups, 16535 9th Ave. N, Plymouth, Minnesota, 55447.

Creative Visualization by Shakti Gawain. Bantam, New York, 1982.

CHAPTER 4: HOUSEHOLD JOBS

Most parents want their children to help with household chores. However, the reasons parents give for wanting help vary from family to family. Before looking at what jobs children can do and how to get children to do them, it is useful to look at *why* you want the jobs done.

Why should children help with jobs?

There are four common reasons why parents want children's help with household chores. These reasons affect what tasks parents require of children and how they encourage their children's participation.

To share the work load. Parents feel burdened by the number of household tasks. They wish for assistance with the unending work. This feeling is particularly true in single parent families where there is often more household work to do than time available. Further, some parents believe that if kids are more involved in running a household, they will make fewer messes.

To learn housekeeping skills. The easiest time to learn household skills is as a child. Children can learn to make beds, do dishes, and vacuum the floor the same way they learn to read, ride bikes, and swim. When children leave home for a job, college, or marriage, they will need to know how to keep their space clean, do their own laundry, make simple repairs, manage their money, and prepare and clean up after a meal.

One young adult remembers, "I was amazed to find out how much Mom did that I didn't know about. When I ran out of shampoo or tooth paste or soap, I couldn't just reach into the cupboard to get another one. I spent my first four months away from home running to the drugstore for supplies."

One young woman recalls her embarrassment at not knowing how to do laundry. "I hung around the laundry room trying to find out how to wash and iron clothes because I didn't want others to know how ignorant I was. I was amazed to find how easy it was."

To contribute to the family. Many parents believe that all family members should contribute to the family as well as receive from it. The way each person contributes will vary with age and ability. One way children can contribute is to do household jobs. This approach is illustrated by Anne.

When I was a child, she recalls, we all helped clean. Each person had a job, and we knew it was important. On Saturday we each did our jobs—

Mom did the laundry, Dad tidied the house and took out the trash, Tommy vacuumed the house, Sarah cleaned the kitchen, and I cleaned the bathroom. From time to time we would exchange jobs.

To learn responsibility. Many parents wish to use household chores as a way of teaching responsibility. They believe that children are developing lifelong habits toward responsibility. This belief can be seen in one Dad's recollections.

As a child, I hated to do the dishes each night and mow the lawn each week. When I found that no amount of complaining or excuses would reduce the work, I learned to play games with myself to make the "boring jobs" more tolerable. I still use that approach when my work gets tedious.

How you approach "chores" will affect what your child learns about them. For example, if you wish to teach skills, you will want to set standards and then rotate the tasks when children become competent so they can learn more tasks. On the other hand, if you want to reduce your work load, you may wish to "train" a child to do some things well and leave those tasks to him. Or, if you wish to emphasize family contribution, you may want to get together as a family and list the tasks from which all benefit and decide who will do what. As you decide what you wish children to do, keep your goal in mind.

What is reasonable to expect?

What tasks can a three (six, nine, or twelve)-year-old do? Parents want to know when it is reasonable to expect their children to keep their toys picked up, wash the dishes, or take the trash out. As you may have guessed, there are no simple answers. What is reasonable for each child depends on age, ability, interest, and family structure.

Developing responsibility for household jobs takes time. To prepare for this book I compiled questionnaires about 663 children. Parents indicated which tasks their children helped with and the level of parental support involved for each task. To begin with, children need parental help or companionship to do a task; next, children need reminding or supervision; and finally, they can complete the task alone.

The results of the questionnaires (presented in the Household Jobs Participation Chart on the next page) suggest the process of developing responsibility for household tasks is slow. For example, there are more than six years between the average age children help clean the sink (six years) and the average age they do it without supervision or reminding (twelve years).

Ability increases with age. Looking at the Job Chart, the average four-year-old's involvement is to help others with household jobs, while the average ten-year-old can do many tasks alone. Further, you can see that some twelve-year-old children need to be reminded about tasks they previously did alone. Some children learn more quickly than average and some more slowly, but this chart offers parents a place to start.

Household Jobs Participation Chart

The chart lists common household tasks, the percentage of children involved with the task, and the average age of children at different levels of involvement.

Symbols:
 H means the child needs help with the task,
 R means the child needs reminding or supervision, and
 A means the child does a task as needed without reminding or supervision.

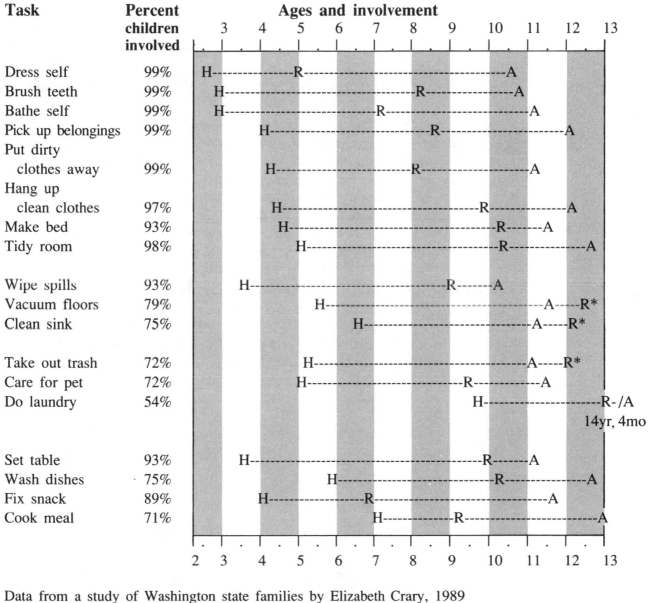

Task	Percent children involved	Ages and involvement
Dress self	99%	H---------------R-------------------------------A
Brush teeth	99%	H-----------------------------R----------------A
Bathe self	99%	H--------------------------------R--------------A
Pick up belongings	99%	H-------------------------------R---------------A
Put dirty clothes away	99%	H-----------------------------R----------------A
Hang up clean clothes	97%	H-------------------------------R--------------A
Make bed	93%	H----------------------------------R------A
Tidy room	98%	H-----------------------------------R-----------A
Wipe spills	93%	H---------------------------------R------A
Vacuum floors	79%	H--------------------------------A----R*
Clean sink	75%	H-----------------------------A----R*
Take out trash	72%	H--------------------------------A----R*
Care for pet	72%	H------------------------R------------A
Do laundry	54%	H---------------------------R-/A 14yr, 4mo
Set table	93%	H---------------------------R------A
Wash dishes	75%	H------------------------------R---------------A
Fix snack	89%	H----------------R-------------------A
Cook meal	71%	H--------------R----------------------A

Data from a study of Washington state families by Elizabeth Crary, 1989
*Children require supervision again after becoming independent

Consider a child's preferences when deciding on tasks. Some children like doing the same job over and over, while others like variety. Some like to work outdoors, while others prefer indoor jobs. Children are more likely to cooperate when they feel as though they are listened to.

We were having a lot of trouble getting our children to do their Saturday jobs. All we heard were complaints, complaints. One evening I listed all the weekly tasks on file cards and briefly described what was involved with each one. Then I asked family members to choose what they wanted to do.

I was amazed. Each of the children took harder jobs than they previously had. Further, they did their new jobs with a minimum of complaint. Now, when the kids complain about their jobs, I ask if they want to trade with someone.

Consider a child's ability. A child's physical build and experience affect what jobs he or she is capable of. For example, much as ten-year-old Amy wants to mow the lawn, she doesn't have the muscle power to control the mower. Experience can influence allocation of children's household tasks two ways. If a child is experienced, she is more likely to be asked to do a job. However, unless children have the opportunity to practice, they will not become experienced. This dilemma is illustrated below.

In my family I have a bit of a problem. William, my oldest, does a good job with everything. Ellen and Sam do tasks less well. This is due, in part, to lack of experience. I used to ask William to do most of the work, because he did it well. One day he complained that he was overworked and thought he should do the job poorly so I wouldn't ask him.

I thought about it and decided he had a point. Now, if company is coming and I want the bathroom cleaned fast and well, I will still ask William to do it. But normally I rotate the jobs so Sam and Ellen also get a chance to learn.

Family situation. If your family is very traditional, with household jobs divided by gender, then you probably would not assign meal preparation to your son or mowing the lawn to your daughter. However, if you want all children to know what is involved in running a household, you may choose to rotate your children through all the tasks. If you are a single parent with

Different sized jobs for different sized kids.   Pick Up Your Socks

one child, you may need to ask that child to do a wider variety of tasks than otherwise. Your family situation and beliefs will affect both the tasks you want done and the way you approach them.

How to teach a task

Teaching any task involves four steps: deciding what you want done, introducing the task, establishing standards, and motivating children to learn.

Decide exactly what you want done. This is the first step in teaching any job. When you say, "set the table," what does that mean? Does it simply mean putting the plates, glasses, and silverware on—or does it include napkins, tablecloth, serving utensils, condiments, and a center piece?

Next, collect the material the child will need. In some situations, that means pointing out where to find items and making sure the child can reach the supplies. In other situations, it means collecting the necessary items and storing them together.

Introduce the task. Remember to consider your child's preferred learning style and match your style to his. For example: You could *show* the child how to set the table (visual), *tell* him how (auditory), or *do* it with him (kinesthetic). You can practice identifying teaching styles in Exercise 4-1.

EXERCISE 4-1: Identifying Teaching Styles

Instructions: Read each of the following situations. Decide which learning style was used to introduce setting the table and what the clues were.

1. Draw a picture of how the table should look. Then, set the table showing her as you go. "Take a plate [show a plate] and put it here. Next, take a fork [show a fork] and put it here ... ."

    Style   *Clues*

2. "First, take the plates and put one at each place. Next, take the forks and put one to the left of each plate ... ."

    Style   *Clues*

3. "I will give you what you need and let you put them in the right place. First, put one of these [give child three plates] at each place. Next, put a fork [hand child the forks] beside each plate here [moving child's hand to left side]."

    Style   *Clues*

Answers:
1. *Visual. Showed* child what to do.   2. *Auditory.* Primary instruction was words.
3. *Kinesthetic.* Involved the child in *doing* the task from the beginning.

Establish a time frame. When parents want something done, they usually have a time frame in mind. If you don't have a particular one in mind, it may be helpful to make one. Otherwise, the task may be put off until the parent gets angry. Some examples are "table set by 5:30," "the leaves raked up before lunch at 12 noon," "your room cleaned before you can invite friends over," or "the trash taken out before you watch *any* television." When you establish a time rule, think about how you will enforce it. If your child does not clean her room, you may have a bored child on your hands. If your child is required to watch a television program for school, will you let her?

Establish standards for the job. Conflicts often arise because a child does not understand what the parent wants. For example, does "make your bed" mean making hospital corners, removing all wrinkles, fluffing the pillow, and tucking the bedspread under the pillow, or simply pulling the covers and bedspread up over the pillow? If you are not clear about what you want, it will be difficult for the child to do it.

The standard needs to reflect both what is reasonable for a child and what you, as a parent, can stand. Sometimes parents will assign a task and then redo it when the child's performance is not satisfactory. That approach teaches a child she can be sloppy because someone else will finish things up.

With younger children, you can identify five parts of the task—one for each finger (see Illustration 1). For example, "clean your room" means: make your bed, hang up clean clothes, put toys away, throw trash away, and put dirty clothes in the hamper.

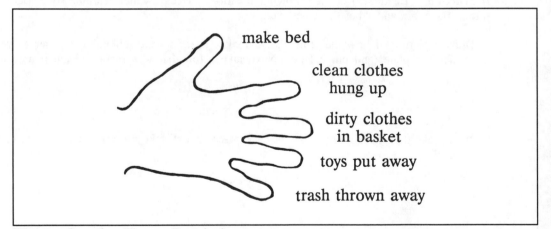

make bed

clean clothes
hung up

dirty clothes
in basket

toys put away

trash thrown away

Illustration 1: Finger Reminder

With older children you can provide a job score sheet (see Illustration 2). Children can score themselves and then you can check them. Most children also enjoy scoring their parents. They could score you on how clean you leave the kitchen or how nicely you keep your room.

Reminder systems

Most people need help starting a new habit—whether it is flossing their teeth, exercising, or noticing kindnesses done to them. Three ways to remember a task are: (1) make a chart; (2) ask someone to remind you; and (3) associate the task with something else you do.

Pick Up Your Socks

Bedroom Score Sheet

Each item earns 1-5 points. 5 points will be awarded for an excellent job. If 40 points are earned you get a special treat. If you do not earn 40 points, you may reschedule the inspection or improve the score the next time.

Date: ____ ____ ____ ____ ____ ____ ____

Bed made ____ ____ ____ ____ ____ ____ ____

Half of floor picked up (near window) ____ ____ ____ ____ ____ ____ ____

Half of floor picked up (near door) ____ ____ ____ ____ ____ ____ ____

Clean clothes put away ____ ____ ____ ____ ____ ____ ____

Dirty clothes in hamper ____ ____ ____ ____ ____ ____ ____

Shoes on shoe rack ____ ____ ____ ____ ____ ____ ____

Desk clean & tidy ____ ____ ____ ____ ____ ____ ____

Bookshelf neat ____ ____ ____ ____ ____ ____ ____

Toy shelf neat ____ ____ ____ ____ ____ ____ ____

Floor swept or vacuumed ____ ____ ____ ____ ____ ____ ____

TOTAL POINTS: ____ ____ ____ ____ ____ ____ ____

Comments:

Visual. Using a chart or a calendar is the most common form of reminder. If the chart is also used for some pleasant purpose or as the basis of a reward, it is more effective. One example is a picture like a game board. Each time the child cleans his room (or does some other task you request), he can color in one square. When all squares are filled in, he gets a privilege or treat. Two examples of progress charts are presented in Illustration 3.

Ask for help. Many children find it easiest to be reminded about new tasks. This is fine as long as the child requests the help and does the task when reminded. When adults take on the job of reminding, it is helpful if they have a timetable for letting go of the responsibility. Otherwise, it becomes the parent's job to remember, not the child's. Ultimately, the child needs to be responsible. If you have gone beyond what seems reasonable, talk with the child and ask for an alternate plan.

Physical associations. Some people remember better if they tie a job to something they already do. For example, Danny had trouble remembering to take his house key with him to school until he decided to check for the key every time he went in or out a door. Other people find it helpful to do something physical to remind them.

Andy had a new aquarium. He had earned the money for it and set it up the way he wanted, but he was having trouble remembering to feed the fish. I had been reminding him, but he never wanted to do it when I reminded him.

One evening we sat down and listed all the ways he could remind himself to feed the fish. He decided to tape a paper over the light switch in his room. In the morning, right after he turned on his room light, he would feed the fish. Once he had the habit, he removed the paper from his light switch.

With many children, developing reasonable expectations, taking time to teach the task, and creating a reminder system work wonders. They accept the responsibility and grow. However, some children still have problems.

Consider or establish rewards. Many parents object to *rewarding* a child for something he or she *should* do. Although this is an understandable position, it is not a practical one. Most people, both adults and children, need help beginning new habits or learning new skills. For example, few people can lose weight or give up smoking without strong support from friends and family or from a clinic.

Rewards can be anything the child wants or needs. Common rewards are praise, money, treats, services, time, and attention. You can also encourage children to feel good about their contribution.

When you establish rewards, keep in mind your purpose for requiring help. If you are a single parent, receiving help preparing and cleaning up from the meal might give you a few minutes to read to your children or play a game with them. If you want to emphasize family participation, you might all go out for lunch or biking when all the jobs are done. If you want children to associate work and money, you can pay for jobs to be done. (This sometimes backfires when teens decide they can get more money working outside the home than in it.)

Discuss consequences of failure. Many children test limits and expectations. You can make this process easier for them and yourself by deciding in advance what you will do when they do not do their jobs.

Pick Up Your Socks

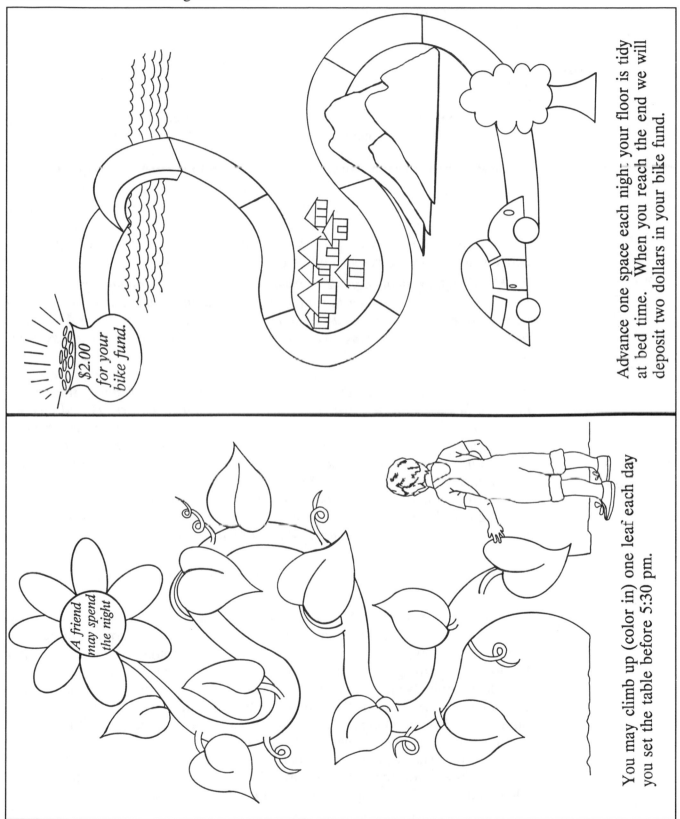

Advance one space each night your floor is tidy at bed time. When you reach the end we will deposit two dollars in your bike fund.

$2.00 for your bike fund.

A friend may spend the night

You may climb up (color in) one leaf each day you set the table before 5:30 pm.

Sometimes the consequence will be the lack of reward; other times it might be withdrawal of a privilege.

"Level Three" Help

Often when parents want their child to do a task alone, they find the child needs supervision or help. A fun way to help children become more responsible is to explain the three levels of responsibilities and ask them what level of work they are doing.

The three levels of help are the same as the three levels of responsibility for tasks presented in Chapter 1. *Level one* refers to needing help or company to do the job. *Level two* refers to needing supervision or reminding. And, *Level three* reflects the ability to do the job without help or reminding. A child who sets the table only if you are present is working on level one. A child who cleans the table promptly when reminded is working on level two. And, a child who gets up from dinner, clears the dishes, and washes them without reminding is working on level three. How one mother used this concept to encourage responsibility is illustrated below.

My daughter Beth, age 12, wished to earn some extra money. I agreed to pay her for pruning the bushes instead of paying a handyman to do it. I was willing to pay her well—assuming she did the whole thing. Later, I found she had quit, leaving twigs and sticks all over. When I expressed my disappointment, she got huffy.

In trying to explain my frustration, I hit upon using the three levels of responsibility. Using gardening as an example, I explained that if she needed me with her to weed, that was level one. If she pulled the weeds and cleaned up when reminded, that was level two. If she checked the garden every other day, removed weeds and composted them without assistance or a reminder, that would be level three. Then I asked her how the levels might apply to the pruning.

When she understood, I told her I would pay her based on her level of work—$1.00/hour for level one work, $2.00/hour for level two, and $3.00/hour for level three. Not surprisingly, she chose to work at level three.

Common problems and excuses

Certain problems or excuses crop up again and again. Following are several issues and possible ways to deal with them.

Unclear job specifications. If a child is taking on a new responsibility, check that he or she understands what the standards are, including timing. For example, Tommy agreed to take the trash out. He thought he did a good job. He took the garbage from under the sink and plopped it in the garbage can outside without being reminded. However, Dad was angry because Tommy did not put a new bag in the can under the sink, nor did he put the lid back on the outside trash can. Dad and Tommy were operating with different expectations. Many problems can be eliminated by clear communication beforehand. That comes with experience and trying some new ideas. With older children, you may wish to have them score you when you do the task. They can use a 1-5 rating system for how well you did the task. You could adapt the bedroom score sheet illustrated earlier in this chapter. With experience, they can develop a sense of how they are doing.

I forgot! Parents could get rich if they received a dollar, or even a dime, for every time their children forgot to do something. There are two possible factors here: the ability to remember and the ability to motivate one's self. Most of the time children do not forget, they just don't pay attention to begin with. That problem can be helped by getting their attention *before* you explain the task. Using one of the reminder systems discussed in this chapter may be enough to help them remember.

A second factor may be a lack of desire to do the task. Many children find that "forgetting" is an easy way to get out of doing things. The best way to deal with this is to help children see that it is in their best interest to do the task. This can be done by adjusting the benefits or consequences (see motivation and consequences). For some children, the desire not to do a particular task is very strong and needs to be addressed separately.

I hate it! Sometimes children find a particular task so distasteful or boring they will not do it. At that point, it is best to review why you want the child to do the task. If you want them to contribute to the family, it may be simpler to find other tasks for them to do. If you want to reduce your work load, again, it could be easier to find other ways they can help. If you want them to learn to do the task, you may be more successful if you wait a while or find some other way to introduce the skills.

Some parents are not willing to reassign tasks because they feel children "should" learn how to do things they don't want to do. If you feel that way, then recognize the issue is "learning to do something unpleasant," rather than contributing to the family or learning a task. If doing the task becomes a family issue, it will take much more energy and supervision on your part to get the child to do the work.

Summary   When children can do a task without help, parents often assume they can be responsible for doing it alone. However, many children are not ready yet because they have not developed the *habit* of doing the task. Unfortunately, developing the habit usually takes much longer than developing the skill. You can encourage the adoption of the habit by rewarding the child when he or she remembers to do it alone.

Additional Reading

401 Ways to Get Your Kids to Work at Home by Bonnie Runyan McCullough and Susan Walker Monson. St. Martin's Press, New York, 1981.

School's Out: Now What? Creative Choices For Your Child by Joan M. Bergstrom. Ten Speed Press, Berkeley, California, 1984.

CHAPTER 5: SCHOOLWORK

School-aged children spend over a third of their waking hours in school. For some children, this time is an exciting adventure in learning; for others, it is a boring, confusing, or humiliating experience. Parents can increase the probability of a good experience by choosing an appropriate school; however, even in a good school, children need skills in *how* to learn, skills to deal with students and teachers, and a learning environment that complements their learning style. Before we consider these aspects of school, we will need to discuss what parents' goals are for their children.

What is the purpose of school?

Although most people want good schools, there is a great difference among parents and professionals about what children *should* learn at school.

Different parents want different things from school for their children. Some parents want their children to learn *information or skills*—how to read, do arithmetic, and have a basic understanding of science and history. Other parents want their children to *get good grades*. They are concerned with getting into college or getting a good job. Still other parents are less concerned with information and more concerned with learning *how* to learn and enjoying it. Some children have no social skills, but easily pick up the academic information they need. Their parents may be more interested in their learning to *work effectively with people* than learning traditional topics. Some parents really don't care much about what their children learn as long as they *stay out of trouble*. The difference in goals can be seen in the two examples below.

I want my child to do well in school. By that I mean to get good grades. The key to getting into a good college and getting a good job is good grades.

I want my kids to do well in school, but more important is that they learn to deal with people. People can be brilliant and have all the right answers; but if they can't communicate with others and gather support for their ideas, nothing will happen.

Reward the behavior you want. Do your children act as you want them to? If not, encourage the behavior you want by changing the way you respond to them. For example, if your child is getting so-so grades, but is learning the information and enjoys school, your actions should reflect your values. If you value grades primarily, then you might want to help the child find ways to improve her grades. If, however, you value *learning* for learning's sake, then you might want to talk about what she is learning and let the grades continue as they are. Exercise 5-1: Identifying School Goals for Children, will help you recognize what you value in school.

The ideal student, for most schools, is one who is mildly curious, persistent, physically quiet, and can concentrate with both noise and quiet. He or she is not affected by the environment and can learn easily from both written and spoken material. Few people combine all these traits. Each person has his or her own individual learning style. The preference for physical and personal conditions has more effect on learning than people once supposed.

Learning preference

Each person's individual learning mode is composed of his or her environmental preferences, temperament, social orientation, learning orientation, and physical makeup. We will look at each of these in turn.

Environmental preferences. Regardless of age, IQ, or achievement levels, people respond individually to their environments when they study. People are influenced differently by sound, light, temperature, and formality of their

---

EXERCISE 5-1: Identifying School Goals for Children

Instructions: Read each of their statements and mark how you feel about it. **E** = Excited, **P** = Pleased, **S** = So-so, **C** = Concerned, **U** = Upset.

Your child —	E	P	S	C	U
1. made the honor roll.	[ ]	[ ]	[ ]	[ ]	[ ]
2. was voted room president.	[ ]	[ ]	[ ]	[ ]	[ ]
3. was caught cheating.	[ ]	[ ]	[ ]	[ ]	[ ]
4. received the only A in math.	[ ]	[ ]	[ ]	[ ]	[ ]
5. is a quiet, cautious, C student.	[ ]	[ ]	[ ]	[ ]	[ ]
6. won the city spelling bee.	[ ]	[ ]	[ ]	[ ]	[ ]
7. comes home and "plays" with the ideas he learns in math.	[ ]	[ ]	[ ]	[ ]	[ ]
8. wants to go to summer school to study biology.	[ ]	[ ]	[ ]	[ ]	[ ]
9. calls a school friend to discuss a joint project.	[ ]	[ ]	[ ]	[ ]	[ ]
10. hit another child on the playground.	[ ]	[ ]	[ ]	[ ]	[ ]

Comments: Numbers 1, 4, & 6 focus on good grades; numbers 7 & 8 on learning; numbers 2 & 9 on social skills; and numbers 3, 5, & 10 on trouble.

surroundings. *Sound* affects people differently. Some people need absolute quiet to concentrate, while others need background noise to work well, and still others can block noise out when they want to. This difference appears to be a physiological one, and is difficult to change.

Some people need bright *light*, others get fidgety and nervous when the light is bright. Some people have trouble concentrating when the *temperature* is too high or low for them. Even the *design of the room* affects learning. Some children study best sitting upright in a chair or at a desk. Others learn better lounging on a bed or the floor. What this means in practical terms is that when you tell a child how to study, you may well be misdirecting her. Parents and teachers need to help children identify and create their best learning environments.

Temperament. There are nine temperament traits (mentioned in Chapter 1) that are relatively consistent throughout childhood. Four of these traits directly affect learning. They are persistence, distractibility, physical sensitivity, and orientation to new situations. Children who have high levels of persistence can stick with an assignment until it is complete. Children who are easily distracted by sights, sounds, or changes in their surroundings will find learning more difficult. Further, some children resist anything new, whether it is a substitute teacher, a new topic, or a change in routine. These children can adapt, but it takes energy that otherwise could be used for learning.

Although temperament traits tend to be consistent over time, children can be taught ways to adapt. For example, easily distractible children can sit where the distractions are fewer. Children who don't like change can look for ways the situation or new person is like a familiar one.

Social orientation and learning. Some people like to learn *alone*, away from the distraction of other students, teachers, or parents. Some children like to learn in *small groups*. They like brainstorming, case studies, and group projects. Other children like to work directly *with an adult*. Still other children do best with *instructional media* like computers, film strips, and videos.

Most topics can be taught many ways. For example, reading can be taught by permitting a child to take a book and ask questions as he needs to, by letting groups of students read plays aloud, by working with one child, or by using computer programs.

You can get an idea of a child's social preference for learning by listening to what subjects or projects the child likes and how they are taught. Then you can ask a teacher to try using more of that style, or arrange for your child to learn outside of school.

Learning orientation. This aspect refers to the general ways people like to approach learning. Some people like to get an overall picture before they start. This approach is called the *global* or "big picture" orientation. Global learners are interested in general relationships. Other people are not at all interested in the big picture and want to start immediately with the parts that make up the whole. This *analytic* or detail approach is often used to teach classes like math and biology. Analytic learners like to know exactly what is expected—how many words the paper should have, where the teacher wants the heading. A third orientation is the *swirl* approach. This approach works on a subject from one direction for a bit and then backs off and approaches the subject from another direction. To some people, switching focus appears confusing and to others it is more interesting. Exercise 5-2: Global-Analytic Style Check List may help you identify your preferred style.

Physiological elements. A person's physical makeup also influences his or her learning style. The *learning channels* or styles, mentioned in Chapter 1, have a physical base. So, also, does a person's *need for movement* or

---

EXERCISE 5-2: Global-Analytic Style Check List

Instructions: Read each item below and check it if it is usually true for you.

Style one	Style two
Do you:	**Do you:**
[ ] use the first idea that comes to your mind when you are solving a problem?	[ ] read for the idea, often skipping words or ideas you don't understand?
[ ] find it easy to concentrate on detail?	[ ] want to understand what is going on (overall) before you start to work on the details?
[ ] finish one task before going to the next?	[ ] have to write the whole paper before you can make an outline for it?
[ ] want to know exactly how an assignment will be graded?	[ ] like to relate what you learn to your own personal interests and experiences?
[ ] prefer a teacher who does not talk much about what he or she has done?	[ ] feel better about completing something if you get a reward or praise?
[ ] become upset when a letter grade is not given on a test or homework?	[ ] ask others' opinions before deciding when you are not sure what to do?
[ ] make most decisions only after considering the problem carefully?	[ ] have a hard time concentrating on one thing at a time?
[ ] want to know exactly what you did wrong?	[ ] dislike being marked down for spelling mistakes on a history paper?

When you finish, count the check marks in each column. You will probably have more in one than the other. The actual number is not important. What is useful is finding your preferred style. *Style one* represents the analytic approach, and *style two* represents the global approach.

mobility. This need for mobility is illustrated in the following woman's observations.

When I first met my husband, I was amazed to watch him pace. When he needed to think or concentrate, he paced—back and forth, back and forth. He stills fidgets when he needs to sit very long. I used to think his need to move was very odd until I realized that my roommate in college knitted while she studied. I don't know how she did it, but she said it helped her concentrate.

When children with a high need for movement are confined to a chair, they often get into trouble or find it difficult to work. For children like these, a classroom that permits movement is essential.

Teacher's impact on learning styles. The closer the match between the student's and teacher's learning styles, the easier it is for a child to learn and get good grades. For example, a student with a global learning style will find it easier to write an essay for a global teacher who wants general concepts and relationships than for an analytic teacher who wants more detail. Similarly, a student with an analytic approach will find it easier to remember the details of a story than to tell the theme or to paraphrase the story. These differences can become a source of growth or discouragement to children depending upon how they are handled.

Coping with different learning styles

When a child's learning style differs greatly from his or her teacher's, there are four approaches a parent can take. First, you can wait and see what happens; second, talk with the teacher; third, offer your child skills to adapt; and fourth, find a tutor with a compatible learning style. Each approach is appropriate at some times and not at others.

Wait and see. If your child feels good about himself as a student, you may want to wait and see what happens. Your child may discover for himself how to adapt to a different teaching style. However, if your child becomes frustrated or discouraged, he will not learn either the subject matter or academic skills.

Kids process information differently. Pick Up Your Socks

Talk to the teacher. Many teachers are interested in helping children learn. If you explain to a teacher what your child needs, the teacher may try to help. The chances are greatest if the request is simple. This is illustrated in the example below.

Martin was having terrible trouble in school. He never seemed to know what was going on and appeared to be daydreaming or bothering his neighbors. This was so unlike him that we set about to find out what was wrong.

He sat in the back of the class and would watch the teacher for a minute or two and then get involved in something that was happening near him. After talking with him and observing the class, I decided that a large part of the difficulty was that Martin was getting distracted by the kids between him and the teacher.

I explained to the teacher that he was easily distracted by what he saw, and asked her to move him to the front of the class. She was willing to try, and most of the problem disappeared. He could hear better, and there was not much to distract him.

Sometimes teachers are too busy or uninterested to help. In those cases your best course may be to teach your child to adapt or to get a tutor.

Adapting to different learning styles. The key to adapting learning styles is to find out what is needed and supply it yourself or to seek it from others. You help children discover how they learn best and how to get the help they need. The following are several ideas you can use or pass on to your children.

Verbal learners. Read instructions verbally to yourself. Talk through the problem to yourself. Pretend you are explaining your writing assignment to someone and write down what you say. Later, come back and tidy up the writing, if needed. If you do not understand the assignment, ask someone (student or adult) to *tell* you what the assignment is or explain to you how to do the problems.

Visual learners. Study in a place with little visual clutter. Read the book. Ask a student or adult to *show* you how to do the problem. Ask the teacher to write important names and dates on the board.

Kinesthetic learners. If you need to wiggle a lot, try to sit where your movement will not bother others. Ask someone to *take* you through the steps of a problem. When you study at home, it may help to move around as you explain things to yourself. If you cannot move around, try wiggling a foot or leg as you read.

Global learners. If you have trouble remembering details, you can make a list of questions you think might be important. You can use questions from your textbook. As you read, look for answers to those questions. Then use a memory aid (described later in this chapter) to associate the detail with the main idea it supports.

If the teacher gives many details, assume they will lead to a whole. Remember the general ideas and relate them to each other.

Analytic learners. If you have trouble grasping the general idea, skim reading assignments for the main idea. Ask yourself "What is this about?" Then go back and read for details. If you have trouble during class, you can ask a friend, who views things globally, to explain the main idea. Make a game of trying to tie the ideas together.

Additional ideas for adapting to different learning styles are presented in the section on basic school skills in this chapter.

Find a tutor. If a child is behind or unable to adapt quickly, it may be helpful to find a tutor with a compatible learning style. Sometimes tutors are available through schools, other times through independent sources. Find someone who is aware of different learning styles and has experience teaching in the ways your child finds easiest to learn.

Basic school skills

Many people consider "reading, 'riting, and 'rithmetic" the basic skills. I would like to add three more skills to the list—"recording assignments," "scheduling time" so work gets done, and "learning how to learn."

Record assignments. This task has two parts—*figuring out what the teacher wants* and *recording all needed information*. Find out when the teacher gives assignments (beginning, end, or middle of class), and how the teacher gives them (telling the class or writing on the board). If the student does not know, he can ask another student or the teacher. In addition, the student needs a system for recording assignments. It can be a sheet in a notebook or a page in an assignment book. Children need to record the date assigned, date due, and any other instructions the teacher gives. Then the child must bring the record home and use it. One father describes his experience below.

Schoolwork, or lack of it, hit a crisis point when Tammy was 12. She got good grades when she did her work, but "when" was the operative word. She much preferred to think about her friends than pay attention in class. After several tries, we finally devised a system that worked for us.

Tammy had a special notebook for class assignments. She was to write her assignments down each day as she got them. If there was no assignment, she was to write that down. Then she had to bring the notebook home each day. Her mother or I could ask to see it any day.

If the record was not current for that day (or she had forgotten the book), she was grounded from social activities (and calls) until school the next day or for 24 hours on the weekend.

Schedule time to work. Most educators suggest that families set a regular study time each day for their children. Although that is a good idea for most children, keep in mind that well before children graduate from high school, they need to learn to plan time themselves. The approach you take to homework should reflect your goals for your child and what your child is like. Below are four different approaches, each with some advantages and some limitations.

Formal schedule. *Our school recommends that children spend one hour a night studying. On week nights from 7 to 8 pm is "study hall." If a child has no homework, she can read a book or practice an approved skill, like typing. If someone has an activity (like scouts or soccer) that conflicts with study times, he needs to make alternate arrangements in advance.*

***Grade dependent.** As long as our son maintains an adequate grade point average (more A's than B's), he can do as he wishes. If his grades drop, he must put in a minimum of an hour a night studying. He can choose when, but it must be done before he watches television. If he doesn't want to watch TV, he needs to begin studying an hour before his bedtime.*

***Planning oriented.** We really want our kids to be able to plan their time well. We often discuss our plans with the children. Each evening, we ask about their assignments and whether anyone will need help. Sometimes Jennifer will want help studying spelling words or Peter will want his math assignment checked. When they were younger, we used to help them guess (plan) how much time different assignments would take. Jennifer discovered it would take her all evening to learn her spelling if she waited until the last day, but a total of 40 minutes if she did 10 minutes a day.*

***Relaxed.** I believe that if a child is going to get good grades he must do it for himself. I stay completely out of the homework issue. That is between Jason and his teacher. He doesn't get as good grades as I think he can, but he knows he is in charge of what he learns.*

Learn how to learn. Learning information has two parts: process and content. Many people believe knowing how to find and use information is as important as memorizing the facts and figures themselves. Each person needs to learn his or her own way.

I learned in high school that I could cram for a test. Unfortunately, if I memorized something, it was gone very quickly. Several years later I learned to 'organize' the material. Somehow the process of organizing helped me learn the material in a way I could remember.

Adapt to different learning styles. Many people have a particular method they think students should use to memorize spelling words or other facts. If, however, children differ in learning styles, then the parent's or teacher's effort will be more effective if children are permitted to learn in a way that is easiest for them. The following three ways to learn spelling words illustrate how adults can adapt to children's learning styles.

Visual approach. Children write a word and look at it. They should pay attention to both the letters and the shape of the word. (For example, *hook* and *book* look similar.) Next, they imagine the word in their minds and then write it on paper.

Verbal approach. With the verbal approach a child says the word and then spells it out loud. Sometimes it is helpful to sound the word out, but that can also be confusing. If the child can develop a rhythm for the word, it will be easier to remember. The classic example of this is spelling the word "Mississippi." Once most children have learned the rhythm of "mIssIssIppI," they remember it.

Kinesthetic approach. Some children learn most quickly by incorporating movement into their learning. For example, if a child misspelled the word "rhythm" as "rythm," he could practice spelling it correctly by clapping one time as he says *r*, then snapping his finger as he says the *h* he forgot previously, and clapping once more for each of the remaining letters y-t-h-m. For kinesthetic children, doing something physical helps them remember the word. And doing something physically different helps them remember the difficult parts. These three types of learning can be adapted to math facts and other situations. You can practice identifying different learning styles and adapting information to the child's needs in Exercise 5-3: Adapting Learning Styles.

EXERCISE 5-3: Adapting Learning Style

Instructions: Read each situation. Identify the learning style, and suggest how a parent might respond.

Situation 1. Molly was having trouble with math facts and word problems. Mr. Roberts, Molly's teacher, suggested using flash cards. We have been practicing with them, but she is not progressing very well. Every evening Molly complains about the story problems saying, "I don't know what he wants. The teacher never tells us how to do the problems."

Style: _____

Suggestion for improving math: _____

_____

_____

Situation 2. Kevin likes to know exactly what he is supposed to do. He can remember facts easily, but this year he finds geography very hard. Ms. Tamiko likes the students to think about relationships. Today she gave them a list of sets of countries or cities and asked which one was different. For example: Paris, Baghdad, Rome, Madrid, and London. Kevin could not figure out what to do.

Style: _____

Suggestion for doing homework: _____

_____

_____

Possible answers:
Situation 1: Verbal learner. Try reading story problems aloud and practicing math facts verbally.
Situation 2: Analytic learner. Before beginning the homework, help Kevin list types of possible relationships. (For example, on the same continent, touching the same ocean, landlocked, or same side of the equator.) Then have him locate the countries or cites and go down the list of possible relationships.

Pick Up Your Socks

Memorization skills. The ability to memorize information is essential for students and professionals. Memorization involves recording data, retaining it, and recalling it. (This was presented briefly in Chapter 2.) To retain and recall information, the data must be organized and associated with something the student will remember.

Record information. To record the information, it must be meaningful and interesting to the student. Hopefully, teachers will present material in a way that is relevant and interesting to students. If not, parents can. For example, fractions are interesting when you divide a pizza among five people or double a favorite cookie recipe.

Retain information. Information is useless unless it is organized in a way that it can be found later. Parents can help children organize material and develop associations. Two common ways to organize material are with a key word or sentence, or by the peg system. These systems help by creating an orderly storage and retrieval process. They also help by making the list more interesting.

The concept of *key word* uses each letter of a word to recall words starting with those letters. For example, the name *Roy G. Biv* represents the orders of the colors in the rainbow: red, orange, yellow, green, blue, indigo, and violet. The key word concept can be expanded to a *key sentence* as shown below.

Matt couldn't remember the order of the planets. We solved the problem by making a sentence with the first letter from each planet: "Men very easily make jugs serve useful needs period." He could then remember—Mercury, Venus, Earth, Mars, Jupiter, Saturn, Uranus, Neptune, and Pluto.

The *peg* system is more complicated, and more versatile. In this system, students memorize a series of pegs, which they will use to organize and recall information. Once students have learned the pegs, they can be reused. Students can create their own pegs or adapt the nursery rhyme "One-Two, Buckle My Shoe." The process is illustrated in the following example.

Vanessa had trouble remembering lists. In order to memorize the first eight presidents, we taught her the peg system. She wrote the number, the peg, and then formed a connection (usually a picture) between the peg and the president.

one	**bun**	*Washing* a bun	*Washington*
two	**shoe**	*Adam* & Eve wearing shoes	*John Adams*
three	**tree**	Peppers on (*Jeffers-on*) a tree	*Jefferson*
four	**door**	A *mad son* at the door	*Madison*
five	**hive**	*Man rowing* a hive out on a lake	*Monroe*
six	**sticks**	*Twins see* sticks	*Quincy Adams*
seven	**heaven**	Playing *Jacks on* heaven	*Jackson*
eight	**gate**	*Van* crashing a gate & *burning*	*Van Buren*

When you help a child with any memory system it is important for him or her to make the connection. Part of the process of memorization is the *creation* of the link.

Practice recalling. Children will find it easier to recall information if you help them recall the information in their preferred learning styles. Ask a visual child to *picture* the information, the verbal child to *say* the information, and the kinesthetic child to *write* the information. When the child can recall the information, switch and ask him or her to recall the information in the same format the teacher will request—matching quiz, oral questions, etc. You can practice thinking of ways to help children memorize information in Exercise 5-4: Memorization Ideas.

EXERCISE 5-4: Memorization Ideas

Instructions: Read the child's statement and suggest a way he or she might memorize the names and locations of all the countries in South America.

1. This is too much. I don't see how I can finish this by Friday. She didn't show us how.

Clue: _____

Suggestion: _____

_____

2. I can't do this, 'cause I can't find my map. It is too hard anyway.

Clue: _____

Suggestion: _____

_____

3. This is a dumb assignment. How does he expect us to learn where the countries are if he doesn't tell us which country is which? He said it would be easy, but I can't tell how to begin.

Clue: _____

Suggestion: _____

_____

Possible answers:
1. *Clues*: "see," "show" indicate visual. *Suggestion*: Look at South America in the encyclopedia. Look at each country. See how it is shaped. Look at the name. See how it is spelled. Imagine the shape of the country and the spelling in your mind.
2. *Clues*: "find," "do" indicate kinesthetic. *Suggestion*: You can find another map in the encyclopedia. You can draw a copy. Find each country and write the names down on the map. Practice doing that again and again.
3. *Clues*: "tell," "said" indicate verbal. *Suggestion*: Read the names of the country out loud. Listen to the words and imagine how they are spelled. Say the name over and over and describe the country to yourself.

Pick Up Your Socks

Ways to help children motivate themselves. Ultimately children must learn to motivate themselves. However, when children are learning a new skill, it may be most effective to help them. Children usually have problems when they find the task overwhelming or extremely boring.

Make task appear manageable. Establish a goal, divide the task into small pieces, collect support for the task, do the work, and reward yourself. (This approach was presented in Chapter 2.) The following example illustrates this process with schoolwork.

Beth (6th grade) was panicked by her first big report. She was to research a topic; write the information in five chapters (each at least a page long); include a table of contents, bibliography, glossary, illustrations; and write a description of the author. She found her resources and began writing note cards, but writing the report seemed overwhelming.

I helped Beth divide the remaining tasks. We came up with: finish reading one book and making note cards; read and write note cards for another book; decide on sections and outline the material; write draft of one section; write two more sections; write the last two sections; type text into computer; create a table of contents, glossary, etc.; draw her illustrations; revise the report and print it out.

To reward her work, Beth wanted a special set of doll clothes. We got the set and I wrapped each item separately. When she completed each step, she could open one package. The surprise of what she would get next encouraged her to keep working.

Make work fun. Help children find ways to make repetitive work interesting. The following list of ideas was suggested by children:
- *I race against myself.*
- *I see if I can get my 4-times-table to beat my 3-times-table.*
- *When I have to write spelling words in sentences, I make the silliest sentences I can think of.*
- *I alternate reading social studies, which is boring, and a new book. Five pages of fun for one page of social studies.*

Common homework problems

There are homework problems common to many children but these are not insurmountable. Possible solutions are discussed below.

Not having the assignment. Help children develop a system for recording assignments. To encourage them to use it, establish a reward and continue using it until they develop the habit of using the system. (Some reward ideas were presented in Chapter 3.) If children can have free time by forgetting assignments, there is no advantage in remembering the assignment.

Not understanding the directions. Children often have trouble with the directions for an assignment. Two common reasons exist—first, the student did not read the directions carefully; second, he or she has difficulty understanding instructions visually. If the child rereads the instructions and they are still unclear, ask him to read the instructions *out loud*. If he still has trouble, ask him to point to the part he has trouble with.

Math errors. Children can dramatically reduce errors by doing math assignments before they are tired and checking that they copied the problems correctly. Most students do best when they write down all their computations (even what they do in their head) and check their work. Writing down the problem and the information is particularly important in story problems.

When the homework is done, you may want to check the work and point out errors. After a while, you may be able to detect a pattern in the type of errors. Gradually, turn responsibility for checking the work over to the student. First, mark individual errors, then just mark the line an error is in, and, eventually, the number of errors on the page.

Writer's block. Many people freeze up when required to write. Most writers agree that writer's block has little to do with laziness or lack of interest, and lots to do with fear: fear of the blank page, fear that what they write will not be as good as they want, fear that it might be really good and people will expect them to do it again, etc. Professional writing guides offer several suggestions that work equally well for students and professionals. Among the ideas are:

Set up a space for writing. Choose a place with few distractions. For example—quiet, but not too quiet. Keep all the writing materials and research tools there—pencils, paper, eraser, dictionary, notes, even a glass of water if necessary. Arrange things so the student can sit down and start immediately.

Begin with a rough draft of ideas. Many people get stuck trying to write perfectly the first time. Most writers find it helpful to write the ideas as they come and *then* go back and make sure the flow, grammar, and spelling are correct. It is helpful to write on every other line (or every third line) so changes and corrections can be made easily.

Write in the order the ideas come. If the only thing you can think of falls in the middle of the assignment, fine. Write the pieces in the order they come. Later, go back and organize them. If a child writes each section on a different sheet of paper, it will be easy to reorganize.

Write every day. Writing is easier when it is done each day. A momentum is created. With adults, 15 minutes of writing is recommended. With

Schoolwork doesn't have to be "Greek," if your child knows how to translate.

Pick Up Your Socks

children, five minutes may be enough. Children may find it easier to start writing about things they know or enjoy. If they are having trouble writing, encourage them to write anything that comes, no matter how silly it is.

Barry Tarshis, in *How to Write Without Pain*, suggests writing at the same time each day. Choose a time when the writer is fresh. The writing period can be extended gradually as the writer gains confidence.

Talk out ideas. Some people find it easier to "tell" what they want to write to someone, before they write. A parent can write (or type) the ideas initially. Later, let the child talk into a recorder and write the ideas down herself.

Copy a paragraph or page you like. For some people, the act of writing (or typing) will start the words flowing. The student can copy something he or she wrote, or something from a book.

Visualize how the paper should look and write words to make it look like that. Some children may even be able to "see" some words in their mind.

If the assignment is long, *stop while you still have ideas* rather than when you get stuck. Stop after you begin a new section, or list the ideas or points you will make next.

Do something physical. Many people find that when they are stuck, it frees their mind to get up and do something active—weed the garden, shoot basketballs, vacuum the floor, or exercise.

These ideas assume that the student has the information he or she needs to write. If children need information, they can either write what they have and then go look for the information, or they can look for the information first. It is helpful for children to realize that almost all writers, professional and not, have difficulty writing sometimes. The main task, for students and professionals, is to learn how to get themselves started.

Summary   Getting started is a much easier task though when the purpose of school and one's own learning style are understood. This chapter has provided means to examine and adapt learning preferences, to gain basic school skills, and to overcome common homework problems. For further study in this area, additional material is listed below.

Additional Reading

Sensory Integration and the Child by A. Jean Ayres. Western Psychological Service, Los Angeles, California, 1979.

How to Write Without Pain by Barry Tarshis. New American Library, New York, 1985.

Your Memory: How It Works and How to Improve It by Kenneth L. Higbee. Prentice-Hall, Englewood Cliffs, New Jersey, 1977.

Your Child is a Person by Stella Chess, Alexander Thomas, and Herbert G. Birch. Penguin, New York, 1977.

CHAPTER 6: INDEPENDENT LIVING

Most parents want to rear children who are capable of living independently as adults. Some people approach this task very systematically, listing the skills they want their children to have before they leave home. Other people assume, or perhaps hope, that with time the skills will come automatically.

Parents want children to be healthy and safe. They want their children to have the skills to be happy and to manage their resources. The first exercise in this chapter lists skills you may want your child to have before leaving home. Some children pick up these skills easily. Others need to be deliberately taught. Exercise 6-1, on Independent Living Skills, may help you identify skills that are important to you. In this chapter we will look at ways to introduce some of these skills.

Personal safety

Children learn safety habits both by observation and discussion. To encourage your children's safety, you can teach them first aid, safe play habits, and to say "No" to drugs and abuse.

Teach first aid. Children who know first aid are less likely to have accidents than children who do not know first aid. However, the thought of having to give first aid scares many adults, or they may think it is too complicated for children to learn. Actually young children, starting about four, can learn and use first aid skills.

The key to teaching first aid is to make it simple and to review it frequently. The book, *A Kid's Guide to First Aid* by Lory Freeman, is written for children. Her book presents the material in short, story-like pieces. An example of how one child used this book follows.

Ricky was 11 years old and very insistent on being independent. One day, during summer vacation, he was out riding his bike and fell off. When he got home, his mother was gone, and he had blood all over himself.

In Ricky's own words, "I got out the book, [A Kid's Guide to First Aid] and read what it said. It said to use direct pressure and elevation. Since the cut was on the top of my head, I figured it was elevated enough, so I pushed on it. It hurt like heck, but it stopped bleeding."

Develop the habit of safety. Playing and working safely involve thinking about safety when you do something that is new or dangerous. One way to help children develop the habit of thinking about safety is to play "What would you do if ...?" or "What might happen if ...?" For example, "What might happen if—you climbed too high in the tree?" or "leaned out of the canoe to grab the glasses you dropped?" "What would you do if—you fell off the dock or cut your finger?" Although coming up with a good answer is useful, learning to think about safety is even more important in the long run. Even children who are "accident prone" can be helped by making a game of playing "What might happen if ...?"

When I first started a Brownie troop I was not sure I would last as a leader. One girl, Molly, was a delight, but she went from one disaster to another.

In the Brownie ring we began to talk about the safety issues of our activities. What might happen if—you wore long, loose hair near a campfire, or ran through the woods, or walked too close to the person in front of you on a hike? We wanted all the girls, but particularly Molly, to think about safety.

EXERCISE 6-1: Independent Living Skills

Instructions: Look at the following skills. Check those that are important to you for your children to learn before they leave home.

Personal care
[ ] Bathes
[ ] Brushes & flosses teeth
[ ] Cares for own clothing
[ ] Exercises for 20 minutes three times a week
[ ] Eats nutritious meals
[ ] Gets adequate sleep
[ ] Wakes self up in the morning

Personal safety
[ ] Knows first aid
[ ] Plays & works safely
[ ] Says "NO" to peers when appropriate, like drugs, cheating, etc.
[ ] Says "NO" to physical or sexual abuse
[ ] Knows five people to contact for help (some non-family members)

Social skills
[ ] Uses good table manners
[ ] Asks appropriate questions
[ ] Says "please" and "thank you"
[ ] Offers seat to older people
[ ] Leaves other people's things alone
[ ] Recognizes other people's needs and makes room for them
[ ] Is thoughtful of other people's feelings

Meal preparation
[ ] Cooks simple meal
[ ] Cleans up after meal
[ ] Stores leftovers appropriately
[ ] Shops for food

Allowances & money management
[ ] Makes independent purchases
[ ] Budgets money
[ ] Maintains a checking account
[ ] Comparison shops
[ ] Saves money

Emotional maturity
[ ] Recognizes other people's feelings.
[ ] Expresses own feelings appropriately
[ ] Knows several ways to deal with negative comments and criticism
[ ] Knows how to nurture self

Expression of anger
[ ] Recognizes signs of anger in self before "blowing up"
[ ] Distinguishes between his or her own anger and other people's anger.
[ ] Knows how to express anger constructively
[ ] Knows several ways to calm self

I knew we were making progress the day we practiced making fires. The fire was laid, and I asked for a volunteer to light the match. Molly's hand went up immediately and then came down. I remarked, "Molly, you just thought about what might happen. That's great. Now if you still want to light the match, I will show you how to do it safely."

Family safety rules. Each family needs to discuss and establish its safety rules. A list of possible rules is provided in Exercise 6-2. Check the ones that work for you and add any others you want.

Saying "NO" to abuse. Unfortunately, the child who is most at risk for sexual abuse or abduction is the nice, polite, courteous child. When an adult, friend or stranger, approaches a child, she needs to tell him "NO!" in a firm, emphatic way, then leave and tell a caring adult. Polite, obedient children often find it difficult to say "NO" to adults.

Many adults are troubled by how to warn a child to be careful without scaring him or her. Most abused children are abused by someone they know, so warnings about "strangers" are not enough. Yet few people want to teach their children to be suspicious of everyone. One solution is to teach them that it is okay to be rude or "mean" to someone who asks you to break a family safety rule. This approach works equally well for known and unknown people. A list of ways to help your child avoid sexual abuse is provided in the appendices.

EXERCISE 6-2: Possible Family Safety Rules

Instructions: Read each rule. Check a **W** if the rule works for your family; a **C** if it can be changed for your family; or a **N** if it is not appropriate for your family.

W   C   N

[ ] [ ] [ ] 1. Always wear your seat belt.

[ ] [ ] [ ] 2. Always check with parent or babysitter before leaving.

[ ] [ ] [ ] 3. Don't go anywhere with someone unless you have been told to in advance.

[ ] [ ] [ ] 4. Yell, scream, and kick if someone tries to grab you.

[ ] [ ] [ ] 5. Meet me (parent) near the entrance door or gate you came in if you get lost.

[ ] [ ] [ ] 6. Don't climb on tree branches smaller than your wrist.

[ ] [ ] [ ] 7. No more than one friend inside the house when you are home alone.

[ ] [ ] [ ] 8. Hold sharp objects with points or blades pointed away from you as you walk.

[ ] [ ] [ ] 9. Don't poke things into electric toaster, sockets, etc.

[ ] [ ] [ ] 10. In the case of fire, leave the house safely and meet at _____.

[ ] [ ] [ ] 11. Answer the door *only* when a grownup is home.

[ ] [ ] [ ] 12. If you answer the phone when you are alone, say your mom can't come to the phone now. (Don't say your parents are not home.)

[ ] [ ] [ ] 13. It is okay to be rude to ***anyone*** (teen or adult) who asks you to break a family safety rule.

Personal safety issues need to be reviewed again and again. Children need to get in the habit of thinking about what can go wrong and how they can cope. Interestingly, being aware of first aid and safety issues does not keep children from doing things, but helps them think of safe ways to do what they want.

Allowance and money management

Most children have learned how to spend money before they leave home, but few have learned to budget and save money effectively. That is not surprising since only a small fraction of families use a budget. However, people who budget are more satisfied with their income than those who do not. A person's basic approach toward money develops in childhood from the attitudes in his family. We will look at three approaches to money and then present some skills children need.

The dole system. With the dole system, children are given money as the parents see fit. Money is not earned. Parents can give or withhold money as they wish.

The advantage of the dole system for children is they can get expensive items if they can justify the expense or if they time their requests well. The disadvantages are that children do not learn to budget or plan expenses. Also, money may develop a psychological value. Children may equate purchases with love and approval or as payment for staying out of the way.

Earned spending money. Children can earn spending money by doing household chores. As children grow older, the tasks become more complex and the payment increases.

The advantage for children of the earned money system is that they have access to money. They learn to associate money with work and learn to work for the money they want. The disadvantages are that children often decide that everything has a price. Further, most children stop doing household jobs when outside jobs (babysitting, newspaper delivery, mowing lawns, etc.) bring in more money.

Family contribution system. With the family contribution system, children receive an allowance because they are family members. No additional money is given out. Money is not connected to work.

The advantage to children is they get a specific amount of money regularly. They can plan how to spend it. Money does not become a "love" issue. A disadvantage is the allowance is rarely large enough to buy the "real things" that children want. Saving for purchases often fails and children spend the money "foolishly."

Considerations. Before you decide on what approach you wish for allowances and money management, there are several questions to consider.

What is the purpose of the money? Is the purpose to help the children learn to budget money or buy items they need or want?

What is the allowance to cover? Is the allowance just for discretionary expenses and entertainment, or do you expect the child to buy school supplies, gifts, and clothing with it?

How much control does the child have over the allowance money? For example, can it be used to buy candy, guns, firecrackers, or pay a sibling or friend to do his or her chores?

How much money is reasonable for a child to have? That depends, of course, on what the purpose of the allowance is and what it is to cover. It also depends on the age of the child, what other children in the neighborhood receive, and what you can afford.

Create your own approach. Fortunately, you are not limited to the three approaches listed above. Before you decide, look at the approaches used in the families you grew up with. What did you like? What would you like to change? Once you have decided what you want the allowance to do and what it is to cover, you can develop something that suits you. One family's approach follows.

In my family, as children, we were supposed to get an allowance, but never really did. If we really needed something, we could ask for it. Sometimes we got it. I was lucky to earn a lot of money babysitting so I could buy things I wanted.

In my husband's family, they received regular allowances. In addition, they had required jobs that paid extra—like mowing the lawn and washing the car.

In our family, the children receive a regular allowance. They get it as a family member: they are expected to help with family chores, but the allowance is not conditional on task completion.

The allowance increases as the children get older. They get a weekly allowance of thirty cents per year of age up until 12, then it remains constant. It is basically discretionary money, although we encourage (not require) children to tithe from it.

In addition, certain jobs are available when kids want extra money. Further, if the children want something expensive that we think is reasonable, like a bicycle or computer, we will pay half when the child earns the other half.

Money skills. People need to understand that money is a resource which they can use wisely or unwisely. Most children, when they first receive an

Child + work —>   money —>   goal

Pick Up Your Socks

allowance, will go out and spend it. This seems to be true whether the child is three, six, or sixteen. If children have had experience with comparative shopping, planning their expenses, and using a checking account, the adjustment to managing money when they leave home will be easier.

A wise teenager, who had just received a credit card for emergency use, remarked, "I think I see how insidious credit cards are. You can charge something now, planning to pay with the money you get at the end of the month. Then when you get paid and pay your bill, you have nothing left of your paycheck. Nothing! That's awful!"

The ability to understand money and use it wisely develops over time. Exercise 6-3, on Children and Money, helps you decide what items a child's allowance might cover at different ages, and plan when you will want to introduce specific money management skills.   .

EXERCISE 6-3: Children and Money

-- PART 1: Allowances ---

Instructions: Check the items you might include in an allowance at the different ages.

Age				Item
6	**9**	**12**	**16**	
[ ]	[ ]	[ ]	[ ]	*Fun*—money for some things your child may want: hobby items, toys, comics, movies, etc.
[ ]	[ ]	[ ]	[ ]	*Lunch money*—to buy a weekly meal ticket. Or to put in a jar, so he or she can take money out each day.
[ ]	[ ]	[ ]	[ ]	*School supplies*—for example, pencils, erasers, or crayons. You can begin with one item and then add more as the child is successful.
[ ]	[ ]	[ ]	[ ]	*Clothes*—plan to save toward one item, like socks or a shirt.
[ ]	[ ]	[ ]	[ ]	*Grooming*—for example, toothpaste, shampoo, deodorant, or haircuts.
[ ]	[ ]	[ ]	[ ]	*Tithes and contributions*—you can decide on a percentage of income or a specific amount.
[ ]	[ ]	[ ]	[ ]	*Holiday and birthday gifts*—budget a monthly amount and put money in savings.

-------------------------------- PART 2: Money Management Skills ----------------------------------

Instructions: Read each of the skills below. Write the age you think it is reasonable to introduce the skill.

Item	Age	Item	Age
1. Have a savings account	_____	7. Get paid for odd jobs	_____
2. Have own checking account	_____	8. Recognize a true bargain	_____
Receive money for:		9. Save for Christmas presents	_____
3. —clothing each month	_____	10. Save for birthday presents	_____
4. —fall school clothes	_____	11. Save for college	_____
5. —school supplies	_____	12. Pay family bills	_____
6. Budget for expenses	_____	13. Use family credit card	_____

Personal care

Our society says people should bathe and wash their clothes frequently. It is wise to care for your teeth, eat nutritious food, and exercise regularly. Unfortunately, the benefits of these activities are not important to many children.

The challenge of personal care is to help the child develop appropriate habits. This is easy if children care. However, many do not. Some discipline books recommend leaving the child alone and letting the natural consequences take place. It is assumed that the child will eventually choose to be clean. While that may be true, some parents are not willing to wait that long.

I want my children to be able to care for themselves and their clothes. When my son was about 12 years old I decided it was time for him to wash his clothes. It was a struggle to get him to do it each week. Finally, I decided to stand aside and see what happened. Nothing happened. The clothes got dirtier and dirtier. He didn't seem to mind at all. I am embarrassed to say I waited almost three months for him to wash them. I decided it was time to change my approach.

I told him I was going to wash his clothes because they were a problem for me, even if they weren't a problem for him. I also began to comment on how nice he looked when he put on a clean shirt and how good it feels to wear clean clothes. My hope was he would learn to like *clean clothes. Several years later that began to happen. When I was slow doing his laundry, he would come and ask me to wash his clothes. Now (at 17) he does his own clothes all the time.*

The options. There is no sure way to develop personal care habits. The easiest way for children to pick up good health habits is for parents to *model good habits*. However, modeling alone is not always enough. Parents may need to discuss personal health issues and *invite children* to participate. Research has found that modeling and talking about issues are more effective than modeling alone. This may be because together the techniques reach more learning styles or because they clarify the issue. *Rewards* work well with some children, particularly if they accompany a record of effort. Another option is allowing a *natural or logical consequence* for unacceptable behavior. If your children do not wash their clothes, it follows naturally that they will have smelly clothes.

Emotional independence

Some children have only vague notions about feelings. They have learned to ignore them or mistrust them. Before children can learn to cope with their feelings, they must understand the nature of feelings, and distinguish between feelings and actions.

Understand the nature of feelings. The most important concept is that *feelings are neither good nor bad.* Love is often thought of as good; however, when it is expressed by "smothering" a child, it is unhealthy. On

Pick Up Your Socks

the other hand, anger is often thought of as bad, but when it motivates a person to make needed changes in his or her life, it is healthy.

You can begin by helping children develop "feeling words." Children need an active *vocabulary* of more words than just mad, sad, scared, and happy. You can talk about the feelings of people you see or read about in stories. When you share an event in your own life, include feeling words—like embarrassed, pleased, disappointed, lonely, and excited.

As children develop a feeling language, adults can point out that people *express feelings in different ways.* One person may get red in the face when angry, while another gets an obstinate set to his mouth. Parents and teachers can also point out that *feelings change.* For example, "Yesterday you were very angry with Eddie and did not want to talk to him ever again. Today you are friends." They can also learn that *feelings differ*— not everyone feels the same intensity, or even the same way, about the same situation.

Distinguish between feelings and actions. Fortunately, children develop this ability between two and three (see developmental tasks in Chapter 1), however, it can be learned at any time. Adults can help children understand by *clarifying the differences.* For example, "It is okay to be mad, but you may not hit her. Find another way to tell her you're mad."

Adults can also help children by *acknowledging feelings* or by active listening. Active listening involves reflecting both the feeling and the content of the situation. For example, "You feel ignored when your parents pay lots of attention to your little brother." If you find yourself using "mad" or "angry" a lot, look for other possible words. Usually angry feelings follow the original feeling.

Another way to help children understand feelings is to model appropriate expression. One common way to do that is with *I-messages.* An I-message expresses how the speaker feels about a situation. An I-message has three parts: "when"—a non-blameful description, "I feel"—explaining how you feel about the behavior and "because"—why the behavior bothered you. For example, *"When* people leave the kitchen counters messy, *I feel* dumped on *because* I have to clean them up before I can cook." References for learning more about I-messages and active listening are provided in the Additional Readings section at the end of this chapter. You can practice identifying appropriate messages and acknowledging feelings in Exercise 6-4: Acknowledging Feelings.

Nurture yourself. Children need to develop ways to support and nurture themselves. This will enable them to make decisions they believe are right even when those decisions are unpopular. It will also help them to continue doing tasks that are boring or difficult. Two common ways people nurture themselves are with positive self-talk and by doing something they enjoy.

Many people believe you create the world you live in with your thoughts. Self-talk can nourish or weaken a child's self-confidence. When a child says, "I'm too stupid to do this" or "I'm fat and ugly," his or her unconscious mind works to make the images real. *Positive self-talk* involves changing a negative thought to a positive idea. For example, "This is hard" or "This is boring" can become "I will feel proud when I get this done" or "I am making progress. I have already done ...." Adults can help children develop positive self-talk by modeling changing the language they use. This can be seen in Anne's example as follows.

As soon as I heard the smoke alarm I knew what was wrong. The vegetables on the stove were burning again. As I yanked the pot off the burner and disengaged the smoke alarm, I said, "This is ridiculous. I am always burning food!" Immediately, I caught myself and revised the statement

---

EXERCISE 6-4: Acknowledging Feelings

Instructions: Read each sentence. Decide if it acknowledges children's feelings or ignores them. Mark the sentence with an **A** if it acknowledges the feelings. Mark the sentence with a **D** if it disregards the child's feelings. If the sentence disregards the child's feelings, revise it.

_____ 1. It's okay to hate your brother, and you may not hit him.

_____ 2. Don't be scared. The dog won't hurt you.

_____ 3. There is no reason to be mad and hit him. It was an accident.

_____ 4. You won't be lonely when I am gone today. Aunt Alice is here to take care of you.

_____ 5. (At the doctor's office) Yes, shots hurt. If you are scared, you can hold my hand.

_____ 6. Smile. It's not as bad as you think.

_____ 7. Sometimes a new place is scary. You can watch the children until you feel comfortable.

Possible answers:
1. Acknowledges feelings.
2. Disregards feelings. Alternative: Sometimes dogs look scary when they try to make friends. You can hold your hand out for him to smell.
3. Disregards feelings. Alternative: You feel mad Ian knocked your blocks down. You can decide how to let him know you are mad without hurting him.
4. Disregards feelings. Alternative: Aunt Alice is here to take care of you. If you feel lonely, tell her and she will help you decide what to do.
5. Acknowledges feelings.
6. Disregards feelings. Alternative: Looks like you're feeling sad. You decided what you wanted to do, and the situation didn't go that way.
7. Acknowledges feelings.

Pick Up Your Socks

to, "Oops! I did it again, but I am getting better. This week I have only burned food once. Soon I'll have cooking under control."

You can involve children in rephrasing negative self-talk by explaining what you are doing and asking for their help. You can practice rephrasing negative ideas in Exercise 6-5: Positive Self-Talk.

Another form of nurturing yourself is to *ask for a compliment*. A child could say to a friend or teacher, "Tell me something you think I do well" or "Tell me something you like about me." Some teachers adapt this by asking students to write something they like about the "child of the week."

Doing something you enjoy is another way for people to nurture themselves. Most preschoolers have self-comforting devices—thumb, pacifier, or special blanket. As children grow older, they also need to develop ways of nurturing themselves. Some activities school-aged children use are: talking to a friend, reading a book, playing cards, listening to music, practicing ball,

---

EXERCISE 6-5: Positive Self-Talk

Instructions: Read each of the statements below and reword it to make a positive self statement.

1. I am too dumb to learn this.

_____

2. Nobody likes me.

_____

3. This is boring.

_____

4. This is too hard. I can't hit the ball.

_____

5. I am a bad speller.

_____

Possible changes:
1. I need to find someone to explain this to me so I can understand.
2. Terry and Pat are mad at me right now. I guess I'll need to find someone else to play with until they calm down.
3. I bet I can find three ways to do this.
4. I was able to learn to kick the ball for soccer; I can learn to hit a tennis ball.
5. I am learning to be a better speller, *or* Thank heavens for computers and spelling checkers.

or playing with a pet. Eating is an activity that many people enjoy, and often turn to, when they feel bored, lonely, or mad. However, if eating is a person's primary nurturing activity, he or she will probably put on weight.

Choosing happiness. Most adults want children to be happy. However, happiness is an individual choice. Some parents fall in the trap of trying to make their children happy. You can't. You can make the situation more pleasant, but each person decides whether to be happy or not. This is illustrated in the following story.

Marty came home from school miserable. Her friends had given her a hard time at recess, and the bus driver made her sit with the boys. I listened to her distress and then suggested a couple of activities to cheer her up. Nothing helped. Finally, I decided to leave her alone and told her, "It looks to me like you want to be miserable now. If you need some ideas when you want to get happy, let me know." About twenty minutes later, Marty came in and asked to make cookies. I said, "Fine," and she was finished being miserable.

Three approaches you can use to encourage children to choose happiness are to acknowledge their choices, question their choices, or affirm that they will change. For example, "I see you have chosen to be sad today." Or to ask, "You had a tough time. Do you want to let yourself have a bad day or do you want some help making it better?" or "I see you are feeling sad now. When you want to feel better, come to me." If a child continually chooses to be angry or sad, you may want to teach him or her ways to reduce anger and frustration, or check to see if something is going on that causes the anger, like a bully or competition.

Anger-management skills

Anger in itself is neither good nor bad. Sometimes, however, people get so involved with being angry that they either become more angry, or forget to move on and resolve it.

Make a decision. Unresolved anger continues to eat at a person. That unresolved anger sometimes causes a person to become ill, short tempered, or grumpy with others. This is described in the three examples below.

William had a substitute teacher for two weeks that his classmates did not like. At first, I ignored the complaints that she was mean. However, after William started coming home with bad stomach aches, I discovered she would ridicule children who got the wrong answer and keep the restless kids in at recess. Although William was not directly involved, he was furious she was so mean.

Whenever my dad has trouble at work you can tell. He gets mad at my sister and me. He doesn't say anything directly, but he gets very brusque and very precise. Nothing we do is good enough.

I can tell when Katie has had a rough day at school. She slams the door, throws her stuff down on the floor, yells at the cat, and picks a fight with her brother. All this before she has been home three minutes!

Situations like the last two usually increase anger and frustration unless the person "yelled at" realizes he or she is not at fault and lets it pass.

Two decisions a person can make are: *do something* about the situation or *let go of the anger*. Both of these approaches work well.

Resolve the situation. If a situation happens again and again, one may wish to do something to change the situation or prevent it from happening again. Do something constructive rather than fretting about what you wished you had done. Two examples:

Kevin was having trouble with some of the older kids on the bus. He had tried ignoring them, but they were getting more and more physical. Our house lies between two bus routes to school. Kevin arranged with the principal to switch buses. An added advantage for him turned out to be that the second bus left 10 minutes later in the morning.

(Patti, age 12) I really don't mind doing the dishes. What I mind is doing lots of dishes because people can't remember what glass they used for a drink or snack. So they use another and another. Everyone agreed to keep track of their glasses, but they didn't. I was getting mad every time I did dishes. I considered refusing to do dishes unless people remembered which glass was theirs and reused it. Then I had an awesome idea. I asked Mom to buy four plastic glasses, each a different color, for people to use. It worked! Now all I have is one extra glass per person.

Let go of anger. Another way to deal with anger or frustration is simply to let go of it. This can be useful when you have looked at your options and decided that the effort to change is more than you wish to expend. In fact, recent studies have shown that letting go of anger is more effective in reducing stress than trying to suppress it or talking about the situation without resolving it. "Letting go" means simply letting the anger disappear or drift away. Simple as the idea is, some children have trouble letting go of anger.

Different people develop different ways to let go of anger. When you offer children ways to reduce anger or frustration, offer a variety. One way

Independent Skills   *Letting go of anger.*   85

to do that is to offer several ways for each learning style—auditory, visual, or kinesthetic. An *auditory* method might be to record their feelings on tape and then discard it or listen to soothing music. *Visual* ways might be to imagine the feelings draining out of you, or to imagine yourself in a calm place and the calmness growing within you. *Kinesthetic* approaches might be to blow out the feelings, or shake or wiggle them out. It is helpful to offer children a variety of ways so they can find what works for them.

Dealing with peer pressure

Somewhere between the ages of six and sixteen, children become interested in friends. One task of school-aged children is to learn that it is okay to believe and act differently from one's friends. Children are learning this skill when they resist peer pressure. The pressure may be for something illegal, like drugs or stealing; something dishonest, like lying or cheating; or due to different values, like partying or status clothes. In dealing with peer pressure, a direct approach usually works best. If a child gives obvious excuses or puts off making a decision, peers will continue to pressure him or her. Four approaches are: be blunt, refer to a parent, get an ally, and bargain.

Be blunt. One way to combat pressure to do something illegal is to call it by its legal term. For example, if a friend wanted your son to take a candy bar (or record) without paying for it, he might reply, "You're crazy. That is shoplifting. I could get arrested for that." If the friend said no one would notice, he could respond, "I could be arrested for shoplifting. I can do without that kind of trouble," and then leave.

Refer to a parent. Another way to resist illegal acts is to say, "I can't do that. My dad (or mom) would kill me." If the friend says that they would not find out, the child could repeat, "You don't know my dad, he finds out everything. He would kill me," and again leave. Some parents agree to support any excuse or reason kids give why they can't do something illegal or questionable.

Get an ally. Peers often try to make others feel as though everyone else does "it," whether "it" is smoking or cheating on a test. With this approach a child or teen names someone else who won't do "it." For example, "I'm not going to. It's not right. Terry and I are going to do ... instead."

Bargain. If a child has something (an item or skill) the other child needs or wants, he or she can use it to bargain.

Teresa was a teacher's aide for math class. That means she corrected papers and entered the grades in the teacher's grade book. She often helped her friend Emily do her homework assignments. One day, when Emily had not completed her assignments, she asked Teresa to record a good grade for her.

Teresa said she could not, but her friend continued to beg, "Come on, be a good sport. No one will ever know." Finally, Teresa said, "No! I won't change your grade. And if you ask me again, I won't help you with your homework for the rest of the quarter."

These techniques have been used successfully by many children and teens. If children have experience thinking about ways to resist pressure before they

EXERCISE 6-6: Resisting Peer Pressure

Instructions: Read each situation and suggest two ways the child could respond.

1. "Come on Frank. Don't be a spoil sport. Give me the matches so I can light the paper. They won't see us. The school needs a little excitement. It won't hurt anyone."

A. _____

_____

B. _____

_____

2. "Debbie, I have great news for you. You have been elected to our new club. In order to be a member you must prove you are a brave and loyal member. To prove you are brave, you must sneak something out of Old Town Store without Mr. Town seeing you."

A. _____

_____

B. _____

_____

3. Nick and Pete have some exciting plans for this evening, and they want Matt to join them. Nick explains, "Guess what I have—some old eggs Mom was going to throw out. They're rotten or something. We can throw them at grumpy, old Mr. Smith's house." [Pause] "What do you mean, 'No'? I'll bet you can't hit Smith's door with an egg. What's the matter, you scared to try?"

A. _____

_____

B. _____

_____

Possible answers:
1. *Blunt approach.* "No way, man. That's arson. You could be arrested for that even if no one is hurt. I don't want that kind of trouble." OR *Bargain*: "No. You may not use my matches. If you ask me again, I won't help you study for the history test tomorrow."
2. *Blunt*: "Lynn, you can't be serious. That's shoplifting! The Golden Girls won't want any of their members to do that. If they do, count me out. I can do without that kind of trouble." OR *Refer to parent*: "Forget it. My dad would be so mad he'd kill me."
3. *Refer to parent*: "My mom would be livid. She'd murder me. You should have seen how mad she was when we soaped his window." OR *Get an ally*: "You're crazy. Egging a house is vandalism. I have a new video movie I'm going to watch. How about it, Pete, do you want to see the video?"

Independent Skills

need them, it will be easier to use those techniques when they are needed. Exercise 6-6: Resisting Peer Pressure can be used by adults or children to practice the four approaches presented. Children can get further experience thinking about peer pressure by reading the Decision Is Yours books: *Finders Keepers*, by Elizabeth Crary, and *Bully on the Bus*, by Carl Bosch.

Summary   In this chapter we have looked at personal safety, money management, emotional independence, anger management, and resisting peer pressure. These skills can be taught by modeling and discussion of options, but rarely by lecture. Some books are listed below if you wish additional references.

Additional Readings

A Kid's Guide to First Aid by Lory Freeman. Parenting Press, Inc., Seattle Washington, 1983.

Without Spanking or Spoiling: *A Practical Approach to Toddler and Preschool Guidance* by Elizabeth Crary. Parenting Press, Inc., Seattle, Washington, 1983.

Parent Effectiveness Training by Thomas Gordon. Peter H. Wyden, Inc., Publisher, New York, New York, 1970.

Dance of Anger: A Woman's Guide to Changing the Patterns of Intimate Relationships by Harriet G. Lerner. Harper & Row, New York, New York, 1985.

Bully on the Bus by Carl W. Bosch. Parenting Press, Inc., Seattle, Washinton, 1988.

Finders, Keepers by Elizabeth Crary. Parenting Press, Inc., Seattle, Washington, 1987.

CHAPTER 7: PUTTING IT TOGETHER

My experience as a parent suggests there are two kinds of challenges in rearing children: nagging problems and intense problems. You can distinguish between the problems by how you *feel* about the behavior, rather than the behavior itself. Nagging problems are often annoying, frustrating, exasperating, but they are not maddening in the same way intense problems are. Parents often feel intensely about problems that are not really serious. When that happens, the problems need to be dealt with as deliberately as if they *were* serious.

When you face a nagging problem, you can amble along trying one possible solution and then another. However, when you find yourself facing a situation that continues to upset you, it is helpful to deliberately consider your options and develop a plan. This chapter will focus on how you, as a parent, can develop an approach to problems that are frustrating to you. We will begin by looking at what parents want for their children in general, then developing teamwork between parents, developing a plan for dealing with the behavior, taking care of yourself, and where to go if you still have trouble.

Where are you coming from? Three factors affect how effective a parent is with the skills he or she has: recognizing values, developing reasonable expectations for children, and accepting yourself. These factors are as important for parents of school-aged children as they are for parents of toddlers and preschoolers. We will look at each of these briefly.

Clarify your goals. When parents do not know what they want for their children, they often feel dissatisfied with their child's behavior without knowing why. Clarifying goals helps parents distinguish between long-term and short-term goals for their children. Also, when you want your child to be responsible, but have no clear idea about what that means to you, it is difficult, if not impossible, to develop a plan. Exercise 1-6, in Chapter 1, looks at identifying your values, and Exercise 7-1, on the next page, looks at ranking children's traits that are important to you.

Develop reasonable expectations. Knowledge of what you want must be balanced with what is possible for a particular child. Children's behavior varies greatly between different ages, and between different children of the same age. This may be due to maturation, personality, or experience.

EXERCISE 7-1: Ranking Children's Traits

Instructions: Rank the personality traits listed below. Use 1 as the most important to you.

_____ ACTIVE, lots of energy, always moving (1)
_____ AGGRESSIVE, competitive (2)
_____ ATHLETIC, does well in sports (3)
_____ ATTRACTIVE, physically nice-looking (4)
_____ CHEERFUL, pleasant, friendly (5)
_____ CLEAN, neat, uncluttered (6)
_____ COORDINATED, physically coordinated (7)
_____ COURAGEOUS, stands up for his or her own beliefs (8)
_____ CURIOUS, inquisitive (9)
_____ FLEXIBLE, resourceful, innovative (10)
_____ FRUGAL, conserves resources and energy (11)
_____ GENEROUS, willingly shares with others (12)
_____ HELPFUL TO OTHERS, altruistic (13)
_____ HONEST, truthful (14)
_____ INDEPENDENT, self-reliant (15 & 25)
_____ INTELLIGENT, intellectual (16)
_____ OBEDIENT, compliant (17)
_____ PASSIVE, not aggressive (18)
_____ PERSISTENT, has "finishing power" (19)
_____ POLITE, well-mannered (20)
_____ POPULAR, liked by peers (21)
_____ RELIGIOUS, respects God (22)
_____ SELF-CONTROLLED, self-restraint (23)
_____ SENSITIVE, considerate of others' feelings (24)

Note: The traits in this exercise focus on the same values as the behaviors presented in Exercise 1-4: Desirable Children's Traits. The numbers in parentheses refer to the corresponding statement in Exercise 1-4.

Developing teamwork

It is easier for children to understand what is expected of them and to learn new behaviors if their parents work as a team. Parents can expand the team to include other adults who work or live with the child; for example, a non-custodial parent, teacher, or day-care provider. Children need clear messages about what is expected of them and what will happen if they do not meet those expectations.

Pick Up Your Socks

Share your goals for your children with each other. Values and goals are neither right nor wrong. Sometimes parents find themselves working at cross purposes because each assumes the other values the same characteristics and behaviors. You can reduce this frustration for all concerned by discussing your goals with your spouse. An easy starting place is to exchange answers for Exercise 1-6: Identifying Your Values, or in Exercise 7-1: Ranking Children's Traits.

Recognize conflicting goals. Although it is simplest if both parents agree on values, it is not necessary. However, parents do need to decide together how to deal with the differences. Otherwise it is confusing for the children. This conflict is illustrated in the following mother's experience.

Marie (age six) did not want her grandmother to come to her family birthday party. Her response surprised me because she usually enjoyed being with Grams. When I questioned Marie as to why she did not want her grandmother, she said, "Because Grams gives bad presents. The clothes she gives are awful." I was astounded and horrified by Marie's response.

When I recovered my breath, I asked why it was so important to get good presents. Marie replied, "It's not the present, it's the trouble. Grams always asks if I like the present. If I say, 'Yes,' I feel bad because Daddy says you should never lie. And, if I say, 'No,' you get mad because it hurts Gram's feelings."

Conflicts can arise between many values. For example, children may feel torn between the pressure to be independent and to be obedient, generous (share things) and frugal (conserve their money and possessions), creative and conventional, aggressive and sensitive, and so on. Once parents have identified a conflict, they can begin to develop ways to reduce their child's stress.

Plan how to deal with differences between values. There are several ways to handle differences between values. One way is to acknowledge that the parents differ and to permit the child to choose between them. Another way is to clarify situations where each value has priority. A third approach is to offer the child some strategies for using both values. These differences are illustrated as they apply to Marie's parents.

Parents choose one approach	*Parents can look at their values for children and make some joint priorities. Mom and Dad could decide that "Honesty is <u>always</u> the best policy," or they could decide that "Kindness is the best policy." Mom and Dad would then explain their joint decision to Marie.*
Parents negotiate priorities	*Marie's parents could explain that in some situations honesty is more important and in others, kindness. For example, in matters of safety and family rules, honesty is expected no matter who gets mad or upset. In other situations, a "white lie" might be permissible if nobody is hurt.*

Offer child skills	*Teach tact and diplomacy. Marie could respond to the gift, "I'm glad you remembered my birthday," or find something about the gift she liked. For example, "I like the color (or texture) of the fabric." Marie could also keep her grandmother informed on how her interest in clothes changes.*
Let children choose	*Parents could tell Marie that both honesty and courtesy are important, and that sometimes they conflict. When they conflict, "We trust you to decide what to do." Parents agree to accept the child's choice.*

When parents are clear about what they desire, it is easier to communicate that to children. If parents cannot agree on what they want, it is unreasonable for them to expect a child to figure it out. Sometimes differences in values or parenting styles turn into a power struggle between parents; when that happens it is helpful for parents to address that issue directly themselves or to get outside assistance to resolve their conflict.

Reduce barriers to teamwork

Children find it easier to grow and change when rules are clear and consistent. Children may take advantage of differences between parents by "forgetting" to tell the second parent that the first parent just said, "No" to the same request, or by telling the second parent the first said, "No" in hopes she or he will reverse the previous decision. Neither approach is healthy for the family. Parents find it easier to develop and implement family rules when they work as a team. Next, we will look at some reasons parents give why they do not offer a united front and some ways parents can begin to work together.

Reasons couples are not united. Parents sometimes explain that they don't have time to talk, or the other person doesn't listen or doesn't want to be involved. Although the explanations may be true, they are the starting point of developing teamwork—not the end. We will look briefly at ways to deal with each.

92   *Someone always loses in a tug-of-war.*   Pick Up Your Socks

Not enough time to talk. Many parents find it difficult to make time to talk in the hustle of modern life. However, if developing teamwork is important to both parents, they can find ways to make it happen. Kelly solved the problem with her busy husband as follows.

Peter, my husband, is a physician. When our kids were very young, he would come home after evening rounds and play with the kids for a bit before they went to sleep. As his practice grew, he began to stay at work longer and longer until the kids hardly saw him except on weekends.

I felt very resentful and angry about always making and enforcing all the decisions for our kids. And I was mad that our kids rarely got to see their father. I tried to talk with him when he got home, but I was so tired or angry that a reasonable conversation was not possible.

After several unsuccessful attempts to discuss the problem with Peter, I developed a plan that worked. I made a date with him two weeks in advance, when he was not on call. Next, I made babysitting arrangements for the children. Early on the morning of our date, I packed a lunch and we went for a picnic all by ourselves.

I explained I needed help making decisions and the kids needed to see their dad. He agreed there was a legitimate problem, but didn't see any solutions. He explained that he needed to write up his notes after evening rounds and by the time he finished, the kids were in bed. We spent an hour and a half brainstorming, and finally came up with an approach that worked.

Peter decided that he could come home immediately after evening rounds and play with the kids for a bit or put them to bed. Then he would write up his notes. During that time I would not interrupt him. When he was done, we could talk.

Some parents find they can talk at home, others find they are distracted and need to get away from home to discuss family issues.

We don't agree on anything. Sometimes when parents make time to discuss parenting issues they find they have very different ideas on how to rear children. Sometimes differences arise from different goals for children, sometimes from different backgrounds, and other times from misunderstanding the other parent's point of view.

One way to begin to deal with differences is to understand where the other person is coming from, and find some common concern. Exercise 7-2 lists questions that may increase understanding between you and your spouse.

When you have identified areas of difference and areas of agreement, you can begin a joint plan. The plan may include compromise, negotiation, or agreement to disagree. *Compromise* consists of choosing a position somewhere between the different beliefs you support. Compromise is illustrated in the following example where parents establish the bedtime routine for their children:

Sandy, my wife, believes children should go to bed every night at the same time. She believes it builds discipline and helps children go to sleep. That

EXERCISE 7-2: Couple Communication Questions

Instructions: Answer the first question and then exchange your answers with your parenting partner. Repeat, exchanging answers after each question. This may be done in an evening or over several days.

1. Five qualities I believe most important for a child to have are:

    a.

    b.

    c.

    d.

    e.

2. Three things I liked or disliked about how I was parented as a child are:

    a.

    b.

    c.

3-A. Three things I like about my parenting are:

    a.

    b.

    c.

B. Three things I like about your parenting are:

    a.

    b.

    c.

4-A. Three areas I could improve in my parenting are:

    a.

    b.

    c.

B. Three areas that concern me about your parenting are:

    a.

    b.

    c.

5-A. Three ways I can support your growth as a parent are:

    a.

    b.

    c.

B. Three ways I would like you to help me grow as a parent are:

    a.

    b.

    c.

is fine for preschoolers, but when children get to be school-aged they need to learn to go to bed when they feel tired.

We compromised by establishing regular bedtimes for school nights (Sunday through Thursday) and open bedtimes on vacations and non-school nights.

A second way to handle differences is *negotiation*. Each person agrees to support a position different from his or her's and receives support from his or her partner on another issue where they differ.

Carolyn and I have many areas where we differ. I grew up on a farm, and family chores were the top priority. I think our kids should clean their rooms, take out the trash, help with supper, and mow the lawn. Carolyn believes schoolwork and music lessons are the top priority. She doesn't want to enforce a lot of rules she doesn't believe in. Somehow the children never have enough time to complete the chores that are important to me.

We finally agreed on a joint priority: homework, two specific chores, practice music, remaining time is then free time.

A third way to deal with differences is to *agree to disagree*. With this approach, each parent is responsible for implementing a plan for his or her

Sample answers for the Couple Communication Questions

1. Qualities important for a child to have: high self-esteem, respect for others, personal discipline (persistence), flexibility, honesty.

2. Things I liked/disliked about the parenting I received: I like that I felt loved and respected; I wish I had learned how to end things—when to quit a committee, leave a job, or throw out junk.

3-A. Things I like about <u>my</u> parenting are: I am realistic about what our children and I can do. I am creative/flexible in finding ways to meet my needs and my children's. I can divide behaviors I want to change into small manageable pieces.

  B. Things I like about <u>your</u> parenting are: You hold high standards. You are a tremendous resource for answers about the world and answer questions with patience. You are learning more and more ways to deal with unacceptable behavior.

4-A. I could improve my parenting by—spending more time with my children doing things that are fun for all of us, learning more about what teens are like and need, following through more consistently with the rules I make, and using different language or expressions for when I am angry than when I am mildly annoyed.

  B. I am concerned that you—bring frustrations from work into your parenting, have standards which are sometimes too unrealistic, and sometimes get mad and make quick decisions/rules that are hard to enforce.

5-A. Ways you can support my growth—Encourage me to do more *fun* things with our children (for example, do the dishes one evening, so I can play a game with the girls). You could volunteer to go with me to a class on "living with teens." Remind me to set a timer so I can check on a child when I said I would. Tell me when you think I look angry so I can check my expression and feelings.

  B. Ways I can support your growth—I can ask you what help/support you would like; I can let you work things out between the children and yourself without my intervention; and I can notice when you do things well and let you know.

goals. The plans are shared with the spouse to make sure the parents are not making conflicting demands on their children, but neither parent is expected to enforce the other's plan. However, in some families the problem is lack of involvement rather than difference of opinion.

My spouse doesn't want to be involved. People may be uninvolved for several reasons. Before you can address lack of involvement, it is helpful to get some ideas about why it occurs.

Some questions to ask would be: Has my spouse always been uninvolved? If not, what precipitated the change? For example: a husband may feel left out of the mother-child bond, or become less involved when he starts a new job. Does your spouse feel intimidated by the task? He may be reluctant if the children are step-children or if he did not have a good role model as a child. Does your spouse feel you are too strict or too lenient?

Is there room for two different parenting styles in your family? (Sometimes the primary caretaker gives the impression there is only one right way to do things—his or her way.) Does your spouse feel criticized whenever he or she gets involved?

When you have looked at possible reasons for your spouse's lack of involvement, you can arrange a time to talk with him or her, or you can use the problem-solving procedure described next in this chapter. Remember that you can only make guesses about why another person acts the way he or she does. Sometimes parents can work out differences themselves, other times they need outside help.

Develop and implement a plan

Parents often become accustomed to handling behavior problems in the same way, even if they are not satisfied with the results. One way around that is to take time and look at the problem, and your goals and expectations for children; list options and possible results of those ideas. The steps are described below.

Define the problem. A statement of the problem needs to focus on specific behavior, rather than on the child's personality or general situation. The description should be factual, not blaming. For example, "Kathy is a lazy slob. She leaves a big mess when she watches TV," focuses on the personality, not the behavior. That statement could become, "Kathy does not tidy up after snacks. She leaves apple cores, orange peels, dirty glasses, and paper scraps all around the sofa when she watches TV."

Gather data. Some possible questions to consider for your child and yourself are:

Does she know what is expected of her? Does she understand the standards and the schedule?

Is the desired behavior reasonable to expect for her age? (Check Chapter 4 for average ages for common household jobs.) Has she demonstrated the ability to perform the behavior you want?

How frequently is the behavior a problem? If there are occasional exceptions, what causes them?

Pick Up Your Socks

What benefits does the child get from her current behavior? Does she think the goal (clean room) is desirable?

What other stresses or demands does she currently face? School troubles? Family problems? Recent move?

Have you established consequences for undesirable behavior or rewards for good behavior? Are they carried out regularly?

What problem will be created if she does not adopt the desired behavior? Why is the desired behavior important to you?

How much are you willing to invest in time, energy, or money to develop the desired behavior?

Kathy's father gathered the following data for the described situation above:

Kathy knows I want her to keep her snack picked up, and she has a pretty good idea how clean is "clean." When I ask her to tidy the room, she starts immediately, but soon gets involved in the shows. By not tidying her snack immediately, she gets to keep watching the show without interruption.

The job chart shows that, at 10, half the children tidy their own room when supervised or reminded. So I suppose she is typical. I am surprised though, that it is not until after 12 that half keep their rooms tidy without help or reminding.

Annoying as the mess is, I don't want to invest lots of time or destroy my relationship with Kathy. I have not consistently enforced a consequence or provided a reward for tidying the room.

It is important to me that she cleans up because I am afraid the mess may get ground into the carpet and begin to stick. I'm not willing to accept that as the natural consequence of Kathy's not cleaning up her snack.

Generate options. Most of the time, when people begin to list options, they write down things they already know, then they look at the list and feel disappointed because there are no new ideas. One way to create new ideas is to generate ideas that are silly, impractical, or impossible. When your mind is free enough to think of new, silly ideas, it is also free enough to think of new, good ideas. List at least 10 ideas; 20 would be better.

Kathy's dad came up with the following list of ideas. Some ideas are practical, some are not. Each idea is numbered.

(1) Send Kathy to tidy her mess 30 minutes before bedtime. As soon as the rec room is tidy, I read to her or play a game with her for whatever time is left. If the stuff is not cleaned up in time, no story or game.

(2) Hire her brother, Chad, to tidy up after her.

(3) Borrow a dog that loves garbage to sit beside her and eat what she drops.

(4) Protect the rug with a tarp or linoleum in the area she uses.

Reward her for keeping the room tidy: (5) a ticket for each night the room is tidy. When she gets five tickets we go out for supper or ice cream; or (6) she can get a privilege (like staying up an hour later on the weekend or eating a meal in the rec room); or (7) using something special of mine like my flute or tools; or (8) go rent a video tape; or (9) go on a hike; or (10) have a friend stay overnight.

Invent an alarm that will (11) ring loudly when a snack mess hits the floor, and continue to ring until the item is properly disposed of, or (12) the alarm will turn off the TV until the item is disposed of.

(13) Paint spots on the rug so Kathy's mess won't show.

Develop consequences for leaving a messy room. If the snack remains are not thrown away, (14) No TV the next day. (15) She can have snack only in the dining room or kitchen. (16) Anytime I see something on the rug, she must stop what she is doing and throw it away immediately. (17) She must clean any mess or spills herself before watching TV again.

Evaluate ideas, choose one, and make a plan. Some ideas generated will be more workable than other ideas. Star the ideas you think are best. Cross off the ideas that probably won't work. And look at the remaining ideas to see if there are ways to improve them.

Next, choose an idea, or ask the child what he or she thinks might help. Consider the time and energy each approach will take, and whether it is respectful to the people involved.

When Dad looked at the ideas, there were several he felt were likely to succeed: (1) send Kathy to clean up 30 minutes early; reward keeping things neat with (7) a privilege or (10) having a friend overnight; and establishing a consequence like (14) no TV next day, or (15) requiring her to eat her snack in the kitchen or the dining room.

Reviewing the workable ideas, he felt that a ticket system would be easiest to carry out since he would not have to watch the time as with the early bed call. Nor would he have to deal with her disappointment at night. If the tickets did not work, he could follow up with either of the consequences.

The only remaining details were to make the rules, list the privileges, and make the tickets. Dad decided to ask Kathy if she wanted to suggest privileges and make the tickets, because he felt the process would work better if she was involved. He planned to try the ticket approach for two weeks and then evaluate it.

Implement the plan and evaluate the success. No plan, regardless of how wonderful it is, is effective unless implemented. If you have been weak implementing plans in the past, you can ask someone to help you. Include a specific time to evaluate the success of your plan. If the results are satisfactory, congratulate yourself. If they are not, revise the plan and try again.

When the list, rules, and tickets were complete, they were put in an old cigar box. Dad made a point of going into the rec room after supper to check for progress.

The first three days, Kathy remembered. The fourth afternoon, she forgot. The next day, she remembered again. After the second week, Dad looked at the results and decided it was definitely worth continuing. It was four weeks before Kathy remembered to clean up every day.

Involve children in your decision-making process. In general, the more you involve children in the process, the more likely the project will be a success. That does not mean letting them make the decision alone, but rather coming to a decision that is workable for all people involved.

In the example above, Kathy's father could have involved her earlier. After he had thought of several ideas, he could have explained the problem, checked the data he had collected, and asked Kathy for ideas. Then they both could have evaluated the ideas, starring items they both liked, and crossing out ideas they both disliked. Again, they would need to develop a plan, choose a time to evaluate, put the plan into action, evaluate the progress, and make needed changes. You can use the format in Exercise 7-3 to develop a plan for a concern of yours.

Take care of yourself

Your competence in dealing with other people depends, to a large extent, on how well you take care of yourself. When you feel rested, energetic, and on top of things, you handle situations more skillfully than if you feel tired and discouraged. We will look at ways to take care of yourself by taking care of your body, doing something you enjoy, giving yourself esteem-building messages, developing a support network, and taking responsibility for change.

Take care of your body. To care for your body, eat nutritious food, exercise regularly, and get enough sleep. Many magazines have advice on diet and exercise. The challenge for most parents is finding a way to fit it in with their lifestyle.

Unfortunately, when people are under stress they often stay up late, skip exercising, and grab a bite to eat. This is counter-productive because exercise (particularly long regular movements like running, swimming, or biking) reduces stress.

Do something you like each day. Read, garden, talk to a friend, work on a crossword puzzle—whatever you enjoy. Your well-being is like a reservoir: if you supply love and support to others and do not take any in, you will eventually run dry. One woman describes her experience below.

Just before Jenny, our second child, was born, we moved from the city to a small town because we thought it was a better place for children. However, Don and I continued to commute to work.

Things were fine until Jenny entered school; then I began to fall apart. I was elected PTA Chairperson. My kids started taking music lessons. Both kids were in soccer. Jenny desperately wanted to be in Brownies, but the troop was full, so I volunteered to start another troop.

At the same time the work at my office increased, so I brought some home each night. There was never enough time for my family and for work. I began yelling at Josh and Jenny all the time, and snapping at people at work. Nothing anyone did was right.

Finally, I realized that most of my problems started with me rather than with others. I was giving so much away that I had nothing left for myself. I began cutting out activities and using the extra time for me. The difference was amazing. I still had too much to do, but I didn't lose my cool as much.

Find some time each day for yourself, no matter how small. If you like to

EXERCISE 7-3: Developing a Plan

Instructions: Pick a problem that has been bothering you and follow it through the steps below.

Step 1: Define the problem and the behavior desired.

Problem:

Desired behavior:

Step 2: Gather data.

Average age for desired behavior: _____

What skills does the child have that make the desired behavior possible?

What does the child need?

What approaches have worked in the past?

Step 3: Generate options. List as many ideas as you can. Be sure to include silly ones and ideas you know won't work.

1.	9.
2.	10.
3.	11.
4.	12.
5.	13.
6.	14.
7.	15.
8.	16.

Step 4: Evaluate options, choose one, and make a plan.   If possible, involve the child in evaluating ideas and choosing a plan.

Step 5: Implement the plan and evaluate the success.

read and don't have time to read a chapter, read a couple of pages. If you like flowers and do not have time to garden, stop and smell the roses as you pass by.

Give yourself affirming messages. Everyone, adult and child, needs affirming messages. People need to hear that they are lovable and capable—especially when things are challenging.

Lovable messages acknowledge that you are valuable just because you are you. You don't earn them. They are not conditional on doing things right. You can say to yourself "I like you" or "I'm okay," or look at yourself in the mirror and say "Hi, I'm glad you're here. I'd be lost without you," or "Your needs are important to me."

Capable affirmations acknowledge what you can do or have done. For example, "I am a lousy parent. My kids never do the dishes without nagging," could become "I am learning how to motivate my children," or "Eddie takes out the trash regularly. Now I need to find a way to encourage him to do the dishes."

If you give yourself negative messages, you can replace them with positive ones. These messages can recognize your basic value, or focus on your successes or your ability to change. For example, "I'm too permissive," could become "I am learning to set clear limits for my kids." You can practice changing self-talk in Exercise 7-4.

Anytime you notice yourself feeling unappreciated or powerless, you can change that with self-talk. When you begin giving affirmations to yourself, it may feel strange. That's okay, you can take your own time to adjust to them.

Develop a support network. Everyone needs the support of positive, caring people. If you are surrounded with complaining, critical people, find people you enjoy being with. Some people have friends or family who encourage them to grow. However, it is unreasonable to expect a spouse, or any one person, to fill all one's needs. If you do not have enough supportive people around you, find some. Parenting and self-esteem-building groups offer help with parenting issues. People often form friendships in church or growth groups which offer personal support. Further, you can call an old friend and renew the friendship.

Take responsibility for change. Although most people know how to care for themselves, many do not use that information. The most common reasons for not enjoying one's self are lack of time and too many responsibilities. The Protestant work ethic encourages us to work before we play. People tell themselves they will exercise or do something fun when they have more time—next week, next month, or next year. However, that time never comes.

Identify your priorities. There are several fine time management books and courses available. A classic in the field is *How to Get Control of Your Time and Your Life* by Alan Lakein. Time management systems usually begin by looking at what is important to you and how you spend your time. If you record how you spend time you may be surprised, as Kathleen was in the following example.

I run a small mail order business from my home so I can be with my children. However, my daughter, age six, complained that I never had time for her. When I asked her what she meant, she said, "You are always too busy to do anything with me." As I watched my actions over the next week, I found she was right, so I enrolled in a time management class.

Doing the class exercises, I discovered two things that surprised me. First, I was spending an average of an hour and 50 minutes a day in trips to the copy shop and grocery store. And second, half the time I spent in volunteer work was not important or enjoyable to me anymore.

EXERCISE 7-4: Changing Self-Talk

Instructions: Read each sentence and re-word the statement so it is positive.

1. Why can't I do anything right?

   _____

2. I never learn. I just get in the same mess over and over.

   _____

3. My kids are more aggressive than other kids.

   _____

4. Nobody cares about how I feel.

   _____

5. There is not enough time to do what I need to do.

   _____

6. I have never been good at working with people.

   _____

Possible answers:
1. I do many things well. Today, I got up and got the kids dressed and fed. We ran around the house, and no one has been to the emergency room today.
2. When I am ready, I can get help changing my behavior.
3. Each person is different. My children are learning to handle conflict constructively.
4. I care about my feelings. Teresa cares and so does God.
5. There is enough time for what is really important, or, I can arrange things to make room for what is really important to me.
6. I am learning to deal with people. I am much better than I was two years ago. I set limits for Matty, and I tell Tom how his behavior affects me.

Pick Up Your Socks

Plan your time to reflect your priorities. When you have collected information, you are ready to plan changes. Make a list of all the changes you could make to free up time. Common ways to get more time are to combine trips, lower household standards, delegate to family members, eliminate tasks, and pay for services. After you have listed possibilities, evaluate them, and decide what you will do. Some possibilities for Kathleen are listed below.

I looked at my activities and marked those directly related to my priorities and those I enjoyed. Then I listed ways to reduce time spent on the other tasks and developed a plan.

Combine trips	*(1) Plan grocery shopping so I go once every week.* *(2) Plan swimming lessons and dentist trips so both kids go at the same time.* *(3) Carpool with other parents to soccer practice.*
Lower standards	*(1) Mop floors once a month, rather than once a week.* *(2) Accept small discrepancies when balancing the checkbook.*
Delegate to family members	*(1) Children can fold and put away their clean clothes.* *(2) Each person keeps his or her room clean.* *(3) Each person cleans one room other than his or her own room.*
Eliminate tasks	*(1) Quit volunteer work that is no longer important to me.* *(2) Stop dusting unless company is coming.* *(3) Buy only wash-and-dry clothes to avoid ironing.* *(4) Find music lessons or dentist children can walk to.*
Pay for services	*(1) Hire a high school student to pack orders and help with routine correspondence.* *(2) Pay someone (professional or teen) to mow the lawn or clean the kitchen.* *(3) Pay neighbor to chauffeur kids.*

The two most effective time savers for me were (1) combining errands and (2) resigning from committee work. Now I go to the copy shop twice a week, and grocery shopping once a week. Planning those trips saves me almost eight hours a week (2.75 hours rather than 10.8). It is too early to know how much I will save by not volunteering.

Personal care is an individual responsibility. The best way to teach your child to care for himself or herself is to model caring for yourself. Part of caring for yourself is collecting the information and ideas you need, and part is implementing the ideas you choose. If you consistently forget or are unable to carry through with your plan, you may wish to look at why you let that happen. Often a counselor, or someone outside your family, can give you a new perspective.

What to do if my child still has a problem?

Sometimes parents do everything they know of and still have problems with a child. There are several possible reasons—the child may have organic problems (like dyslexia or allergies) that need to be dealt with, or parents are unknowingly using their information incorrectly. We will look briefly at each of these situations.

Organic (physical and medical) problems. Some children have physical problems that affect their behavior. Children with allergies may act irritable, hostile, and impulsive. Children with dyslexia may have difficulty understanding instructions and remembering things. Children with spatial or tactile defensiveness may require more space and become aggressive when their space is threatened. In each of these situations the physical problems may overshadow typical behavioral growth.

The first step in dealing with the situation is diagnosing it. Some school systems have testing facilities, although many of them require a child to be a year or two behind peers before he or she can be enrolled in special classes. Some traditional doctors are aware of the physical origins of behavioral problems, but many are not. Parents may find it easier to locate knowledgeable doctors with a referral from a counselor or a naturopath.

Behavioral problems. Some problems stem from misuse of information. Each person has his or her own unique way of looking at information. Parents apply information in a way that makes sense to them. Sometimes they unknowingly sabotage themselves. Two ways parents can identify their errors are to participate in a parenting class, where participants practice the techniques presented, or to see a counselor.

Relationship problems. Some children have difficulty because of unresolved problems between adults. Either the child plays parents against one another, or the child exhibits unacceptable behavior to keep his parents focused on him rather than fighting with each other. In either case, the family needs help. Some counselors or therapists specialize in family systems and can help families develop more healthy relationships.

Consider counseling. Some children have problems that are beyond the scope of simple education. These children need counseling and help in reorienting themselves. If you choose counseling or therapy, choose a counselor you feel comfortable with and confident in. Talk with several people before you decide. Remember that the counselor who was great for a friend may not be great for you.

In this chapter we have looked at clarifying your goals, encouraging teamwork between parents, developing and implementing a plan, and how to take care of yourself so you will have the energy to implement the plans you develop.

Where do you go from here?

You're off to try, and try, and try again. No technique works all the time. If it did, life would be much simpler. However, different approaches work at different times. The challenge is to keep trying until you find what works for you and your children.

Responsibility does not magically appear at age 8, or 12, or 18. It is the result of many experiences and the decisions people make about those experiences. Our job as parents and teachers is to establish a framework in which children can grow. You can develop that framework by accepting children where they are and establishing experiences and consequences which encourage them to become responsible.

You can model changing and growing yourself. You have already begun by reading this book and trying the exercises. You can read more about issues that trouble or interest you. You can adapt the material you read to your situations. And you can keep experimenting until you find what works for you and your children.

Additional Readings

How to Get Control of Your Time and Your Life by Alan Lakein. Signet Books, New York, 1974.

How to Put More Time in Your Life by Dru Scott. New American Library, New York, 1981.

The Superwoman Syndrome by Marjorie Hansen Shaevitz. Warner Books, New York, 1984.

Sensory Integration and the Child by A. Jean Ayres. Western Psychological Service, Los Angeles, California, 1979.

TEACHING PERSONAL SAFETY
Summary Sheet

1. Encourage children's self-esteem. Children who feel good about themselves are less likely to develop a "secret" relationship with an adult. Let your child know that you like him or her. Give your child attention.

2. Establish and use a Touching Code with your family. It is easier for children to say "NO" if they have specific words. Children will believe and use the Touching Code only if they see it work, time after time. The code could be "No," "It's *my* body," "Don't touch me," or anything your family chooses. The important thing is that all family members respect it.

3. Acknowledge feelings. Children who recognize and trust their feelings are more able to resist uncomfortable touch. You can model talking about your feelings. Avoid labeling feelings as good or bad—feelings are neither good nor bad. Avoid discounting feelings—"You don't hate your brother," or "You shouldn't feel mad about a little thing like that."

4. Help children relate feelings to types of touch. Children need to be able to recognize feelings as a warning signal. Talk about different types of touch—*good touch* (they like it), *bad touch* (they don't like it), and *I don't know touch* (they are unsure).

5. Give children many chances to make choices. The more experience a child has in making choices, the easier it will be to decide how, and by whom, she wishes to be touched. You can offer choices many times a day, for example, "Do you want to wear your red coat or your blue sweater?"

6. Distinguish between *surprises* and *secrets*. Surprises are private *only* for a limited time. Secrets are used to exclude people and have no end. Abusers want to keep their relationship a secret. They extract a promise from children "not to tell." No adult has a right to ask children to keep a secret from his or her parents.

7. Distinguish between *reporting* and *tattling*. Abusers tell children no one will believe them—because no one likes tattlers. If your child can distinguish between reporting and tattling she will be more likely to report abuse. Reporting informs or asks for help. Tattling tries to get someone in trouble. Encourage children by listening to their reporting.

8. Recognize that familiar people can be abusers. In 75-85% of sexual abuse cases, the child knows the offender. Tell children that no one, friend or stranger, has the right to touch them in uncomfortable ways. Ask them to tell you if they need to use the Touching Code with a grownup or older child.

9. Play "What would you do if ...?" Children who have had experience thinking of what to do in games are more able to think of what to do when molested. Include a wide variety of situations in your games. For example, "What would you do if you left your coat on the school bus? Or if a big kid lifts your dress to see what you are wearing underneath?"

10. Encourage children to keep telling. Children need three or four adults to talk to in addition to their parents. Tell your child which people you think will listen. In most cases, if a child's previous reports have been listened to, he will be more likely to talk to an adult in spite of an offender's pressure not to.

106 Pick Up Your Socks

OFFERING CHOICES
Summary Sheet

WHAT — Offering choices presents children with at least two options and lets them decide what they will do.

WHY — Decision making is a skill basic to self-esteem, problem solving, and responsibility. Children need experience with many kinds of choices.

PROGRESSION

1. **Simple choices.** These are "either-or" choices. "Do you want to wear your blue sweater or your jacket?" "Do you want to turn off the TV or shall I turn it off?"
2. **Multiple choices.** "Do you want to wear your zip jeans, your button jeans, or your new pants?" (Add more choices as your child is able to handle them.)
3. **Ask for possible choices.** "What have you considered wearing?"

FINDING CHOICES

You can use either the logical or creative approach to finding alternatives.

   Creative approach. Look at the situation from a different perspective. For example, ask yourself, how might I solve this problem if I were — a child guidance expert, a magician, someone from outer space, a neighbor, my favorite aunt, a monkey, or the president.

   Logical approach. Adapt each of the following categories to your situation. Some categories are constructive, some are not. When you are generating ideas, the ideas do not need to be practical. In fact, evaluating ideas as you go inhibits the flow of good, new ideas.

Find a substitute:
   -for yourself or the other person
   -find a similar item
   -ask someone for a substitute
   -do a different activity
   -use a different item.

Bargain:
   -offer the use of something special while ...
   -trade for time (read story to other person)
   -trade for service (do other's job).

Make a rule to cover future situations.
   -odd day .../even day ...
   -the first person to ...

Both use the same object:
   -at the same time
   -alternating use
   -wait until the other is done.

Threaten to do something mean or tell on other person.

Get help
   -to intervene for you,
   -for moral support. It can be a parent, teacher, friend, sibling, police.

Distract the other person to a different activity. It is like bargaining, but without the other person's noticing.

EXAMPLE

   Situation: Dawn and William each get one hour of TV time a day. They are quarreling over who gets to sit in the comfortable chair to watch television. Dawn: "You always sit there, it's my turn." William: "I was here first. So, it's my turn." They want you to decide.

   Creative possibilities: *Space man*—hold a child on his lap as he hovers. *President*—make rule that Dawn uses it on even days, William on odd days. *Magician*—make another chair. *Aunt Em*—let the "loser" use her special rocking chair. *Neighbor*—no TV until they find a solution. *Child guidance expert*—help the children solve the problem themselves.

   Logical possibilities: *Both use*: They both sit in the chair together or they alternate at commercials. *Find substitute*: One child can use a stool. *Bargain*: The child who sits in the chair will set the table for the other child next meal. *Get help*: Get a parent to decide whose turn it is. *Make a rule*: The person who is using their TV time gets the chair. *Distraction*: Ask Mom to bake cookies with the other child's help.

   Choose some ideas to try. Select the three or four ideas you think may work and offer them. In this example the children chose to make a rule—the person who was using his or her TV time got the chair.

HELPING CHILDREN SOLVE THEIR PROBLEMS
Summary Sheet

NOTE: *Adult's job*—to help the children remain focused on the problem solving process.

1. GATHER DATA

Collect information about events and feelings. If you plan to help the children negotiate, avoid blaming anyone (even if you think someone is at fault). Some possible questions:

What happened?   How did you feel ...?   How did your friend feel ...?   What did your friend do?   How did you feel when your friend ...?   What happened then?

2. STATE THE PROBLEM CLEARLY

It is easier for children to solve a problem if they have a clear understanding of it. State the problem in terms of both children's needs. You can use one of these approaches or develop your own.

You want to _____ and your friend wants to _____. What can you do so you both can be happy?   **OR**   *I know you are both upset about what happened. Let that pass. I want to talk about some things we might do to make you both happy <u>now</u>.*

Remember: Include both (all) children's needs in the problem statement.

3. GENERATE MANY IDEAS

Go for quantity. Write all ideas down if you can't remember them. Encourage children to suggest silly ideas as well as practical ones.

Write down all the ideas. Evaluate them later. Evaluation stops the creative process.
Encourage different ideas. If a child offers a similar idea, ask for something different. For example, *Hitting, punching, and biting are all hurting ideas. What is something different?*
Avoid criticizing ideas. If a child offers an idea you do not like, help him or her evaluate it in the next step.
Review problem frequently. It is easy for kids to wander from the problem. For example, *Yes, that is a problem too. Right now we are looking for ways to _____. When we are done, we can consider that.*
Focus on the children's ideas. Resist the temptation to add your ideas, unless you are asked. If you offer ideas, they will become dependent upon *your* skill rather than develop their own.

4. EVALUATE THE IDEAS

Consider *all* ideas. The purpose is to help *children* distinguish between good and poor ideas.

Look at the consequences of the ideas. Encourage children to consider the question, *What might happen if you ____?* OR *How will Mary feel if you _____?*
Is this a win-win alternative? Will this idea work for all people involved?
If no idea is acceptable, ask children how to make the ideas more workable.

5. ASK FOR A DECISION AND HELP CHILDREN PLAN

List the alternatives, ask the children for a decision, help them plan how to implement the idea, and decide on a time to evaluate the plan.

List the alternatives. Remember to include all ideas—even the ones you don't like.
Plan implementation. What do the children need to do first? Will the children need someone's permission or cooperation?
Plan time to evaluate. Decide on a time to review the plan and see if it was successful. If the solution is not working, choose another idea or go back and identify the problem again. If the idea was successful ...
Congratulate the children on finding a solution.

Pick Up Your Socks

Index

Help Children Solve Social Conflicts

Jason has a toy. Amy wants it. David can't find anyone to play with him. Kelly is tired of waiting for her turn on the swing. Sound familiar? Of course! All of us have found ourselves in the role of negotiator in our children's conflicts. Children's Problem Solving Books can make that job easier.

Children's Problem Solving Books help children resolve social conflicts.

Research shows that the more alternatives a child can think of the more likely he or she is to display socially acceptable behavior. Elizabeth Crary's books help increase children's awareness of alternatives and possible outcomes of those behaviors.

How to use Children's Problem Solving Books —

These books are different. Each book can be read traditionally (straight through) or as a "choice" book. As a choice book, it invites listener participation. When the story comes to a decision the child can decide what the character will do. The reader then turns to the appropriate page and continues with the story. The text includes questions that encourage children to consider the feelings of others.

Each book focuses on a different issue, offers several alternatives, and illustrates possible consequences of those choices. Each book is $6.95. **The set of six books is sold for the price of five: $34.75.**

I Want It: What can Amy do when Megan has the truck she wants? *Paper 1-884734-14-6*

I Can't Wait: How can Luke get a turn on the trampoline? *Paper 1-884734-22-7*

I Want to Play: How can Danny find someone to play with? *Paper 1-884734-18-9*

My Name Is Not Dummy: How can Jenny get Eduardo to stop calling her a dummy? *Paper 1-884734-16-2*

I'm Lost: What can Amy do to find her dad? *Paper 1-884734-24-3*

Mommy, Don't Go: What can Matt do when he doesn't want his mother to leave? *Paper 1-884734-20-0*

Written by Elizabeth Crary
Ms. Crary is the author of more than 25 books, among them the best-selling *Without Spanking or Spoiling* and *Love & Limits.* She is a parent education instructor at North Seattle Community College and a frequently requested speaker for workshops and conferences across the United States and Canada.

Illustrated by Marina Megale
Within the simplicity of her illustrations, Marina Megale captures the depth and variety of childhood emotions. She has pictured children with both the joy and frustration involved in social situations. Ms. Megale works as an artist in Seattle.

See ordering information on following page.

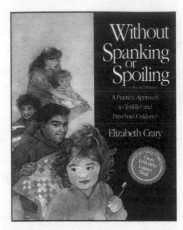